The Stop Overthinking Activity Book
by Nick Trenton

Table of Contents

SECTION 1: MINDFULNESS AND BREATHING — 9

- TRIANGLE BREATHING EXERCISE — 11
- BODY SCAN COLORING — 15
- MINDFUL EATING EXERCISE — 17
- GRATITUDE BREATHING — 19
- VISUALIZATION EXERCISE — 21
- NATURE OBSERVATION — 23
- AFFIRMATION BREATHING — 25
- MINDFULNESS BINGO — 27
- FINGER BREATHING — 29
- LEAVES ON THE STREAM — 31
- RAIN — 33
- PROGRESSIVE MUSCLE RELAXATION SCRIPT — 35
- BELLY BREATHING — 37
- LKM — 39

SECTION 2: CREATIVE EXPRESSION AND PRESENCE — 43

- DOODLING — 43
- CALM-DOWN MANDALA CREATION — 45
- GRATITUDE JOURNAL: THREE GOOD THINGS — 47
- STREAM OF CONSCIOUSNESS WRITING — 49
- VISION BOARD CREATION — 51
- SELF-CARE COLLAGE — 53
- POETRY FOR RELAXATION — 55

EMOTIONS WHEEL EXERCISE	56
GRATITUDE JAR	59
LIFE STORY	61
THE TREE OF LIFE	63
INSIDE OUT/OUTSIDE IN	65
TURNING ANXIETY TO CALM	67
AFFIRMATION ART	70
PICTURE OF ME	72

SECTION 3: PRACTICAL STRATEGIES FOR LIFE MANAGEMENT 75

DAILY TIME MANAGEMENT	75
(GROW) GOAL-SETTING WORKSHEET	77
EISENHOWER MATRIX FOR PRIORITIZATION	79
GENERATING ALTERNATIVE SOLUTIONS AND BETTER DECISION MAKING	82
BOUNDARY-SETTING WORKSHEET	84
DEVELOP A SELF-CARE PLAN	86
TIME BLOCKING ACTIVITY	89
PROCRASTINATION WORKSHEET	91
LOOKING BACK, LOOKING FORWARD	97
HABIT TRACKING	100
DEVELOPING A GROWTH MINDSET	101
SILVER LININGS	105
PERSONAL STRENGTHS INVENTORY	106
REPLACING WHAT IF STATEMENTS	109
FOCUSING ON LITTLE THINGS	111

SECTION 4: SELF-CARE PRACTICES FOR HEALING AND REPAIR — 114

MY SELF-CARE PROMISE	116
NURTURING VS. DEPLETING ACTIVITIES	117
HEALTHY MEAL PLANNING	119
TWO-WEEK SLEEP DIARY	121
MOVEMENT BREAKS	123
DIGITAL DETOX	124
POSITIVE SELF-TALK EXERCISE	127
WRITE A LETTER TO YOUR PAST AND FUTURE SELF	128
SELF-ESTEEM STEMS	130
BIBLIOTHERAPY	132
LEARNING SELF-FORGIVENESS	134
LOSE THE MASK!	136
SELF-LOVE JOURNAL	138
CATCH YOURSELF BEING GREAT	140

SECTION 5: INSPIRATIONAL MINDSETS, AFFIRMATIONS, AND MODELS — 143

QUOTE REFLECTION	143
DEAR ME	144
THE HAPPY NEWS CHALLENGE	146
SETTING RADICAL ACCEPTANCE GOALS	148
SET DAILY INTENTIONS	150
INSPIRATIONAL QUOTE CRYPTOGRAM	152
EXPLORING MY VALUES	154
PERSONAL MANTRA	156
DIY DAILY QUOTE CALENDAR	159

DEVELOPING PATIENCE	**161**
WHEN WAS I (NOT) RESILIENT?	**163**
CULTIVATING REALISTIC OPTIMISM	**165**
PROTECTIVE FACTORS	**167**
IMPROVE THE MOMENT	**169**
POSITIVE JOURNALING	**171**
CONCLUSION	**175**

Section 1: Mindfulness and Breathing

If you're someone who has battled anxiety, worry, and overthinking in your life, then you'll know that sometimes, you just need a quick fix!

Of course, there really are no "quick fixes" in life, but let's be honest–when you're in the middle of an anxiety spiral or trapped in a distressing situation, the last thing you want to do is sit down and focus on reading a complicated book for 45 minutes. And while therapy is undoubtedly effective when it comes to treating anxiety, progress made during a weekly session with a therapist doesn't always carry over into the everyday stresses of life.

So, what can we do?

This is a book designed to cut to the chase. Anxiety can be tricky to deal with, but thankfully there's a lot that you can do, to start cultivating the resilience, self-awareness, and self-love needed to get on top of your worry and overthinking. That's what this book is all about.

Each section has a different focus, but contains 15 complete, standalone exercises that you can quickly use to boost your mental wellbeing and to find a little bit of peace and calm. We'll explore mindfulness techniques, ways to use art to explore our feelings, pragmatic approaches to solving life's problems, self-care tips, and using the power of language to reshape our thoughts and feelings.

Feel free to read the book from start to finish, or to dip in and out as necessary. Some exercises will feel especially relevant, whereas others will need a little tweaking to bring benefits into your unique life. That's OK!

What matters the most is that you are consistently taking some time out to focus on your mental and emotional wellbeing, shifting your perspective, building self-awareness, and pulling your attention to real, practical strategies that will quickly get you feeling better. **Luckily for us, we can start accessing some of these benefits in as little as ten minutes a day**. Commit to a daily practice (say, in the morning), or try out one of the exercises or prompts any time you feel anxiety rearing its head.

One caveat: the exercises in this book are for everyone, and can be adapted as necessary. That said, they are not intended to replace any professional mental health treatment you may require, so use your discretion.

To get started, all you will need is a few quiet minutes to spend with yourself, a journal and pen, and a heaping dose of open-mindedness to try a little something new. Let's dive in.

Triangle Breathing Exercise

It all starts with a breath.

Have you ever noticed how when you're anxious and your mind is going a million miles an hour, your breathing starts to become really *difficult*?

We can imagine that **the breath is a reflection of our state of mind–the way we breathe is the bodily manifestation of our emotional and cognitive reality**. If we are tense, our breath is tense. If we are relaxed and loose, then so is our breathing.

Now, when we are stressed out and anxious, our breathing shows it. The relationship, however, goes the other direction, too: if we can mindfully bring our breathing back under calm, conscious control, then we can affect our emotions and state of mind. Calm, ordered breathing can lead to calm, ordered thinking and feeling.

Even when life feels like it's spiraling and stealing every bit of calm you had, you can still find peace within the storm. The triangle breathing exercise, so simple and yet so powerful, invites you back to yourself. It's more than breathing; it's an anchor. This is your moment of stillness, a grounding pause when everything feels like it's rushing past.

The technique is simple: **Link your breathing to a triangle shape**. Let it create a rhythm that quiets your mind, releasing tension and bringing you home to yourself, slowly and surely.

Visualize a triangle in front of you. If it helps, draw one and trace it with your finger. Start at the bottom left corner. As you trace up the first side, count to six, breathing in deeply through your nose. Feel your chest lift; your lungs fill. Once you reach the peak, hold your breath for three seconds as you follow the right side down, enjoying a quiet moment suspended in time. Let this stillness calm you.

Moving across the bottom, exhale slowly, once again counting out six seconds. Let go of stress, anxiety, pressure. Let it all just drift away. As you return to the bottom left corner, repeat the cycle, inhaling, holding, and exhaling with each traced triangle.

Each breath softens your body, quiets your mind, and settles your spirit, creating an inner refuge. This pattern becomes a gentle wave, pulling you back to center, giving you peace and strength. Triangle breathing isn't just a technique. It's a tool to help you breathe, relax, and find balance when life feels like too much to carry.

Just one triangle at a time.

5-4-3-2-1 Grounding Technique

When life feels chaotic and anxiety starts to creep in, it's easy to feel swept away as worries pile up, each one like a wave crashing, one after another, until you're left scrambling to stay afloat. The feeling is pretty familiar, isn't it?

But there's a way to find your footing: the 5-4-3-2-1 grounding technique. This simple exercise can draw you out of anxious thoughts and back into the present, rooting you firmly in the here and now. By tuning into your five senses, you begin to let go of the swirling worries, finding instead what's real and immediate around you.

There's a reason that this exercise works so well. When we are anxious, our minds are flitting all over the place: to the past to worry about what's already happened, and to the future, to worry about what might happen. **One place the anxious mind usually isn't, however, is the present.**

The mind is a powerful thing, and there is arguably no end to what it can imagine. This is why anxiety can sometimes feel infinite! Endless thoughts can project limitlessly into the past, the future, or some abstract hypotheticals. Untethered to anything, your mind shoots off– and your anxiety shoots off with it.

In the present, however, we are limited. The present is smaller. More manageable. It comes at us much more slowly and steadily. It's *real*.

If we get stuck in our heads, our minds can take us anywhere. **If we stay grounded in the present, however, we slow down and calm down.** We can imagine that the ropes that allow us to tie ourselves more firmly to the present are our bodily senses–sight, sound, etc. As long as we are engaged in the present via our senses, we are not getting carried away by our anxious thoughts.

Here's how to put this idea into practice:

Begin with a deep belly breath. Feel the air filling your lungs, grounding you. Then, start the process.

Five. Look around and find five things you can see. Say each one out loud. "I see my phone, a picture frame, the clock, the window, and my shoes." Notice the details. Let them anchor your mind in the present.

Four. Now, identify four physical sensations. It could be the warmth of your socks, the texture of your clothes, or the coolness of a nearby surface. Say each one aloud. Feel your connection to this moment.

Three. Listen for three sounds. Perhaps the hum of a fan, the ticking clock, or your own breath.

Hearing these sounds, you reconnect with what surrounds you, quieting the noise within.

Two. Notice two scents around you. If none stand out, think of a favorite smell: fresh coffee, lavender, or rain.

One. Find one taste. It might be water, or perhaps the memory of your favorite flavor.

Finish with a deep, grounding breath. Feel yourself centered and rooted in the present. Feels good, doesn't it?

Body Scan Coloring

Our bodies and our minds are connected. The thing that connects them? Breath, and awareness.

It's common to think of anxiety as "all in your head", but it's in your body, too. Become aware of this tension and use your breath to accept and then release it.

Our bodies hold stories—silent, unseen tales woven into muscles, nerves, and breath. Often, we carry tension or emotion without realizing it, feeling the effects yet unable to fully express them. Body scan coloring offers a way to bring these sensations to light, blending mindfulness with creative expression in a calming, active meditation.

To begin, find a comfortable space to sit or lie down and gather paper and your favorite art materials. Start with a gentle body scan to connect inward. Close your eyes and focus on the points where your body meets the ground. Notice the rhythm of your breath, the weight of your feet, and the feeling of being supported. Slowly guide your awareness from your heels, up through your legs, belly, chest, arms, and to your forehead, noting sensations like warmth, tingling, or tension.

As these feelings emerge, imagine colors, textures, or shapes that represent them. When ready, open your eyes, take a deep breath, and let your hand move freely on the paper. Use colors, lines, and forms to express areas of tension or comfort, each mark a quiet conversation between mind and body.

You might, for example, find yourself automatically gravitating towards warm colors like red and orange, or find that your experience is best reflected in jagged lines and sharp angles. What shapes, symbols, or even words express your body's experience right now? Your own creativity is really the limit.

When finished, take a moment to reflect. What did the colors and shapes reveal about your inner landscape? If it feels right, journal about your experience, allowing this creative reflection to deepen your awareness. If this exercise is repeated, you may also get a fascinating longitudinal view on your state of mind and body over time. Notice how certain themes, colors, and ideas repeat–can you detect any larger patterns?

Body scan coloring invites you to listen to your body, nurturing a sense of calm and connection that stays long after the colors fade. If you practice this technique often enough, you may find that you are gradually developing a kind of heightened emotional literacy, and a new fluency in understanding your feelings and the way you articulate your experiences..

Mindful Eating Exercise

Have you ever noticed how easily you can eat a whole snack without truly tasting it? If you're like me, you know that sinking feeling of suddenly realizing that the thing you were eating has completely disappeared, and you can scarcely remember gobbling it up!

Mindless eating happens when we're rushed or distracted, and miss the pleasure that food can offer. Understandably, it can lead to poor eating habits. Eating without conscious awareness can sometimes even lead to poor digestion and overeating, which brings its own stress and discomfort. If you've ever identified with the phrase "emotional eater", then you already know how awful it is to be stuck in a cycle of stress eating.

Mindful eating, on the other hand, invites you to slow down, savor each bite, and fully engage with the experience. The mindful eating exercise is a powerful tool to use in order to reconnect with your food, using each of the five senses to deepen the moment.

First, choose a small snack with a peel or wrapper, like a piece of fruit, chocolate, or a nut, and find a quiet space. Begin by observing the snack's appearance. Notice the color, shape, and texture of its outer layer. Does it have any patterns, marks, or imperfections? After peeling or opening it, look at how the inside differs in color and texture.

How does the outer layer feel? Smooth, rough, or waxy? Then, feel the inside—is it soft, sticky, or juicy? Take in the sensations on your fingertips and tongue. Now listen closely. As you peel or open, notice any sounds that are made, perhaps a snap or a rustle. As you bite, tune in to the crunch or softness.

Smell the snack before and after opening, and pay attention to how its aroma changes. Finally, taste. Savor the initial flavor, then notice how it changes as you chew, enjoying each layer of taste. One thing you might notice is that you can derive immense enjoyment and satisfaction from an eating experience *without* eating a lot. This can be incredibly liberating for those of us who struggle with binge eating.

Even if you do not struggle with binging in particular, a mindful eating practice turns every snack or meal into a calming ritual, grounding you in each sensory detail and making every bite a mindful, enriching experience.

Gratitude Breathing

The anxious mind is filled to the brim with worries. And, when you think about it, worrying is not all that different from *complaining*–we notice and then zoom in on everything that seems wrong in the world, or everything that seems like it could go wrong. While we're doing this, we may be completely ignoring all the wonderful blessings unfolding around us. You may not have thought of it this way before, but **anxiety has a lot in common with ingratitude.**

When was the last time you felt truly grateful?

In a world where it's easy to get lost in what's missing, gratitude often slips through the cracks, leaving us focused on what we lack instead of what we have. Practicing gratitude isn't about ignoring challenges; it's about finding peace in appreciating the small, often overlooked moments. This gratitude-focused breathing exercise pairs mindful breaths with prompts, helping you release tension and embrace a calm, thankful state.

Start by lying on your back, knees bent, feet flat on the floor, and hands resting on your belly. Begin with five gentle breaths, noticing the rise and fall of your belly. Let your body sink into the moment.

Now, deepen each breath through your nose, letting your belly expand as you inhale and contract as you exhale. Continue for 10–20 breaths, allowing calmness to fill you.

Next, move through gratitude prompts with each full breath cycle. On the inhale, think of a prompt, and on the exhale, think of your response. Some examples are:

Inhale: "Something good that happened today was…" Exhale: Reflect on the event.

Inhale: "Someone I am grateful to is…" Exhale: Reflect on why.

Inhale: "A place I am grateful for is…" Exhale: Think about its meaning.

Inhale: "I am grateful for who I am because…" Exhale: Acknowledge a quality.

Inhale: "Something else I am grateful for is…" Exhale: Reflect on the reason.

With each breath, let gratitude settle within, fostering peace and appreciation one mindful breath at a time. It's a great idea to practice gratitude exercises either first thing in the morning, or just before you go to bed at night. In the morning, notice if beginning in a spirit of gratitude helps change your mindset through the rest of the day; in the evening, look back on the day you've had and try to see it all through the lens of thankfulness.

Visualization Exercise

Overthinking, ruminating, and anxious self-talk is basically your brain's habit of telling itself a horrible story–then believing that story!

Turn this idea on its head and realize that you always possess the power to tell yourself a different story. When we overthink and catastrophize, we conjure up a fearful image in our mind, then focus all of our attention onto it until our entire mood and perspective is colored by it.

What would happen if you used your power of visualization in the other direction? What if you used mental imagery to calm, reassure, and soothe yourself?

Sometimes, life feels like a grey cloud hanging over you, dimming everything in sight. Those moments can weigh you down, clouding your thoughts and disconnecting you from peace. Visualization can be a powerful tool to break through, lifting that grey cloud and reconnecting with calm and clarity. By vividly imagining your desires and a place of peace, you direct your energy toward what truly matters, creating a pathway to reach it. It's more than daydreaming; it's a grounding exercise that clarifies your intentions and opens the door to possibility.

Begin with the "floating on a cloud" visualization exercise. Lie comfortably on your back, close your eyes, and take a few deep breaths. Let your body settle and relax each muscle.

Now, picture a fluffy, inviting cloud drifting above you. Imagine its softness, noticing its color and shape. Feel the calm it brings. This is your cloud, a safe haven. Visualize yourself climbing onto it, feeling it support you like a gentle cushion, easing away your tension.

Your cloud begins to lift, carrying you to a serene place—maybe a quiet beach, a lush forest, a starry landscape, or a mountain peak. Look around, absorbing the sights, sounds, and sensations of this peaceful place.

Rest here. Allow worries to fade, embracing the deep sense of calm around you. When you're ready to return, take a few deep breaths and open your eyes, feeling refreshed and light. This fluffy cloud is your mental retreat and sanctuary, always prepared whenever you need a break.

Nature Observation

There are many people who find that nature is their most reliable and available form of therapy. The natural world possesses a quality that can act like a balm for the soul. There is something healing about leaving the man-made world of worries and noise, and entering into a natural realm where things simply are as they are. Where life unfolds at its correct pace, where things have their place, and where everything carries on with life according to its kind. Have you ever noticed how it's only human beings who seem to suffer from anxiety?

Step outside. Notice how the world feels different—fresh air filling your lungs, sunlight warming your skin, and the sounds of nature offering a quiet yet beautiful symphony. Outdoor meditation invites you to blend the calm of mindfulness with the beauty of nature, creating a space to find clarity and peace beyond the usual walls of daily life. In the open air, each breath feels more freeing and each sound more vibrant, helping you feel truly present and grounded in the world around you.

Allow the natural world to slow you down. Look into a serene pool of water and contemplate its surface. Rest with it for a moment. Think about the tree and how it arranges itself. Think about how the leaves at the top of the tree are connected to the soil deep, deep down at the root of the tree. "Nature does not rush" said Lao Tzu, "yet everything is accomplished."

To fully connect with nature, try a mindful walk focused on silent observation. Bring a sketchbook and a drawing tool, then begin by walking slowly and quietly, aiming not to make a sound. Notice the soft rustling of leaves, the warmth of sunlight filtering through, and the intricate play of light and shadow. As you walk, immerse yourself in your surroundings by finding and drawing a few objects, each offering a chance to focus deeply.

Look for something as tall as you are. Observe its shape, colors, and textures, noticing details that make it unique. Then, find something as small as a penny—note its fine details, contrasting it with the larger elements around you. Finally, seek something about the size of your hand. Examine its texture, edges, and weight, feeling its presence in your hands, if possible.

This mindful walk and drawing exercise invites you to slow down and experience nature's special details, transforming a simple walk into a meditative journey of connection and peace.

Affirmation Breathing

How many times have you spoken unkindly to yourself today so far?

Perhaps, negative self-talk is so habitual that you barely even notice yourself doing it anymore.

Negative self-talk can creep in like an unwelcome guest, amplifying doubts and overshadowing your confidence. It almost always accompanies overthinking, anxiety, rumination, and a host of other negative thought patterns.

Affirmation breathing is a powerful way to counteract these thoughts, combining deep breathing with positive affirmations to help anchor uplifting beliefs in your mind. This practice not only quiets negative chatter, but also creates a calm, receptive state where affirmations can truly take root.

Deep breathing alone helps to relax the body and clear the mind, inviting calm and clarity with each inhale and releasing tension with each exhale. When paired with affirmations, each breath becomes a vessel for positivity, turning intention into something you can feel. Visual reminders of your affirmations, like having a list or worksheet in front of you, can help reinforce focus and anchor these beliefs more firmly within you. Practiced consistently, affirmation breathing fosters a sense of motivation, optimism, and grounding.

To begin, take a few deep breaths, inhaling deeply through your nose and exhaling slowly through your mouth, allowing your body and mind to settle. With each breath, invite calm and clarity, focusing on letting go of tension with every exhale. Once settled, start combining each breath with a positive affirmation.

You can combine this technique with other visualization elements, such as imagining those negative thoughts leaving your body as a fine mist or flowing away from you like water. Repeat affirmations either silently or aloud, such as, "I am thankful for...," "I am proud of...," "I am becoming...," or "I am resilient when...."

Remember that the power of **an affirmation is not in the words themselves, but the emotion within those words**. As you speak, try to really *mean* what you say. What would it feel like for you to really, truly believe in the words?

As you move through these affirmations, let each positive statement sink in, grounding your thoughts in gratitude, strength, and purpose. This exercise can help shift your mindset from negativity, bringing calm and empowerment into your daily life.

Mindfulness Bingo

Imagine a classic game of bingo, where each square holds a mix of excitement and anticipation as you mark off numbers, hoping for a win. Now, replace those numbers with moments of mindfulness, small acts that bring calm and awareness to your day, and you have Mindfulness Bingo—a playful way to weave intentionality into your busy schedule.

A fun way to practice mindfulness everyday...

Mindfulness Bingo

Wake up and set an intention for the day	Breathe deeply	Eat deliberately	Speak honestly	Cultivate compassion
Relate kindly to yourself and others	Listen whole-heartedly	Write 3 Good Things about your day before going to sleep	Love fully and allow your heart to expand	Live purposefully, as if Now is all you have
Embody self-love. Practice walking with confidence, or sitting engaged	Listen to, and/or make, music that inspires you.	FREE SPACE	Express yourself: Write your thoughts, draw your feelings, dance!	Take a break from technology
Show appreciation	Take time each day to reflect	Look up from your screen & stretch.	Get lost in the flow of doing what you love	Connect with your senses
Reside fully in the moment, be here now	Think freely and challenge negative self talk	Notice your thoughts without judgement	Declutter one space	Go to sleep 7-8 hours before you need to wake-up

Jennifer Convissor, LCSW, jconvissor@shamesjcv.org

Above is a fantastic example of the way you can lay out a Mindfulness Bingo card (credit to Jennifer Convissor, writing for the The Shames

JCC on the Hudson). You can easily make your own bingo card and make adjustments to include the things you'd most enjoy.

With each square on your worksheet, you're invited to pause, reflect, and savor the present. What's the goal? To check off as many squares as possible throughout the week, turning simple acts into opportunities for growth and peace.

To start, review your Bingo card. Each square offers a mindful activity like "breathe deeply," "set an intention for the day," or "show appreciation." There's no set order; just choose whichever resonates most with you each day. As you complete each activity, mark off its square. Aim for a row, column, or diagonal line to complete a bingo, but remember to enjoy the journey at your own pace. The fun lies in engaging with each moment mindfully.

Remember, each square you marked off isn't just an activity completed—it's a step toward a more intentional, grounded approach to life. These mindful pauses, whether through deep breaths, moments of gratitude, or setting intentions, create lasting shifts in your mindset and energy.

At the week's end, take a few moments to revisit your Bingo card and reflect on the mindful activities you completed. Did taking a moment to breathe deeply help you feel more centered during stressful moments?

A caveat here: Mindfulness Bingo is a fantastic *tool* and a *framework* that helps you cultivate more mindfulness. However, it doesn't work for everyone. If you find yourself getting stressed out about completing everything, or becoming a bit obsessed, it may be that this style of exercise is simply not for you. That's OK!

Finger Breathing

Finding a good breathing exercise can be like discovering a reset button for your day. Five-finger breathing is one of those grounding techniques that offers a quick, accessible way to center yourself when stress or overwhelm creeps in. By pairing deep breaths with the simple act of tracing your fingers, this exercise brings you fully into the present moment, restoring a sense of calm and focus. It is especially helpful in moments when anxiety feels overwhelming, offering a physical anchor to steady your thoughts.

What makes five-finger breathing so powerful is its simplicity. There's no need for special tools or a quiet room—you can practice it anywhere, anytime. It's something you can easily remember, even in the middle of an anxiety spiral. The physical sensation of tracing each finger helps anchor your mind to the here and now, while the deep breaths help calm your body's stress response, leaving you feeling more in control and balanced. You can practice this technique whenever you need to–even in public, for example, by keeping your hands in your pockets or tucked discreetly in your lap.

To start, extend one hand before you, fingers spread slightly. With your other hand, place a finger at the base of your thumb. Inhale deeply as you trace up the thumb's side, then exhale as you trace down the other side. Continue this rhythm with each finger, breathing in as you trace up and out as you trace down, completing a cycle of five deep breaths.

Try to focus intently on the sensation of touch on your skin. Can you feel the tiny ridges and bumps? Just how even and smooth can you make your movements? Can you sync your movements up with each breath? After finishing with one hand, switch to the other and repeat. Each breathe-and-trace cycle brings you back to a balanced, calm state, easing both mind and body. This technique offers a peaceful pause and can be practiced multiple times a day, helping you stay centered no matter what challenges arise.

A modified version is to perform this ritual on just one hand: use the thumb of your hand to trace a line over each of your four fingers. When you reach the end of the pinky finger, simply come back again. This can be especially powerful when you are out walking or simply doing daily errands. As your breath, finger movements, and footsteps all sync up with one another in a steady rhythm, you may find that your mind quiets as well.

Leaves on the Stream

Leaves can be seen as symbols of change, carried away by the wind or floating effortlessly on water. **A leaf is a picture of the transitory nature of life**. A leaf buds, grows, then falls off the tree, only to be followed by another leaf in its place, and then another, season after season. **Thoughts are the same. They arise, then they fall away. Transitory.**

The "leaves on a stream" exercise, inspired by Russ Harris's (2009) *cognitive defusion* techniques in Acceptance and Commitment Therapy (ACT), is about reminding ourselves that our thoughts are not permanent, but as fleeting as leaves. In the exercise, thoughts are visualized as leaves floating peacefully down a stream, helping you create distance from them. You watch as the leaves go, making no effort to hold onto them or stop them. This practice allows you to observe thoughts without attaching to them, reducing their control over your mind and inviting a sense of calm and clarity.

To try your hand at this exercise, find a quiet place where you can sit or lie down comfortably. Close your eyes or soften your gaze, then take a few deep breaths to center yourself. Imagine yourself beside a gentle stream, surrounded by nature's peaceful sounds and colors. Picture the scene vividly to build a soothing mental space.

As thoughts enter your mind, acknowledge each one without judgment. If a task or worry appears, simply think, "I am thinking about [this thought]." Then, gently place that thought on a leaf, setting it afloat in the water. Watch as it drifts down the stream, moving farther and farther from view. Repeat this with each thought, allowing them to come and go without clinging.

Continue this practice for 10–15 minutes, observing and releasing thoughts as they arise. Don't worry too much about visualizing a full, "technicolor" vision that includes all the right details. What matters here is the idea; in whatever way works for you, simply practice becoming aware of arising thoughts, and gently letting them pass again. You might need to change the imagery a little to make it work for you; that's OK!

The "leaves on a stream" exercise encourages gentle detachment, creating mental space and calmness. When practiced regularly, it can help you approach thoughts with greater distance and peace, letting them flow past as you remain grounded and present.

RAIN

Rain isn't just a weather pattern; it can also symbolize the way emotions come and go, sometimes drizzling, other times pouring, but always passing. In the midst of changing weather, we are like the blue sky underneath it all–though our experience changes, the being who is experiencing the change remains constant. The endless blue sky is our unchanging awareness.

The RAIN technique, developed by meditation teacher Michele McDonald and expanded by psychologist Tara Brach, offers a gentle, four-step approach to handling stress and challenging emotions. The RAIN (Recognize, Allow, Investigate, and Nurture) technique helps create a healthy distance from intense feelings, fostering self-compassion and balance.

To use RAIN, start with the first step: **Recognize** what's happening. Notice your thoughts and emotions as they are. Briefly label them—like "I'm feeling anxious" or "This is frustration." Naming the experience begins the process of stepping back, helping you view it more clearly.

For example, let's say you suddenly become aware that you're really annoyed and irritable, and your jaw feels clenched.

Next, **Allow** the feeling to be present without trying to resist or change it. This step doesn't mean you agree with or enjoy the feeling; it's simply about giving it permission to exist. Think of it as gently acknowledging the feeling; "This is here right now, and that's okay."

You may not enjoy the feeling of irritation, for example, but you can accept that this is what is true for you right now. You don't try to force positivity or shame yourself for being irritated.

Then, **Investigate** with curiosity. Ask yourself questions like, "What's really going on here?" or "What does this part of me need?" This gentle inquiry can reveal the underlying layers of your feelings, without judgment or pressure.

You might ask, "What happened to trigger this feeling?"

Finally, **Nurture** yourself with compassion. Offer yourself kindness, whether through a soothing phrase, placing a hand over your heart, or simply allowing a moment of care. Remind yourself that experiencing this emotion is okay, and that you're here for yourself through it.

In our example, you may realize that you are responding irritably to neutral stimuli because you're tired and overwhelmed. You treat yourself with kindness and realize it's time for a break.

The RAIN technique transforms emotional reactions into moments of understanding and self-compassion. Practiced regularly, it builds resilience, helping you remain grounded through life's many storms.

Progressive Muscle Relaxation Script

We've already explored the idea that anxiety is not just something that goes on inside our brains, but rather it's a phenomenon of tension and constriction that occurs all throughout the body.

If your body could speak, what would it say right now?

If your tight shoulders, sore back, or aching head could say something to you, what would they say?

Muscle tension is more than just a physical response-it often reflects the stress and anxiety we carry within. Progressive muscle relaxation (PMR) is a simple yet powerful technique designed to help you release this built-up tension, promoting a deep relaxation that can carry over into daily life. Through this release, we often access healing, greater awareness, and a release of emotional and psychological tension, too.

Through a guided sequence of tensing and relaxing each muscle group, PMR eases the body and calms the mind, providing lasting relief when practiced regularly. Over time, the effects of PMR become more enduring, helping you maintain lower stress levels throughout the day.

Start by settling into a comfortable position and bringing gentle awareness to your body. Starting at the forehead, you focus on each muscle group, moving gradually down to the toes. Moving from one area to the next in a sequence, tense the muscles, hold for about five seconds, and then release, feeling the tension melt away. Repeat this tense-and-release pattern two or three more times. Your relaxation should deepen with each repetition. Deep breathing is encouraged throughout the practice, with each exhale sending a wave of relaxation through your body.

Now, there are many different ways to practice PMR, but the best way to practice will be the way that works best for *you*. Just make sure that you incorporate these key elements:

- Move through one body area at a time, top to bottom or bottom to top.
- Increase tension first, before completely letting go again.
- While tensing, maintain relaxation in the rest of your body.

For example, you might start by raising your eyebrows, holding the tension briefly, and then releasing, noticing how relaxation flows in. This pattern continues through your face, neck, shoulders, back, and down to your legs and feet, leaving you with a thoroughly relaxed mind and body. By tensing first, you access deeper levels of relaxation than if you had merely attempted to relax alone.

Practicing PMR for 10 minutes daily can maximize its benefits, building resilience against stress and cultivating a steady sense of calm. Try to incorporate PMR into your daily bedtime routine, or during breaks in the workday.

Belly Breathing

When we're anxious, our breathing tends to become shallow and rapid, sending signals to the brain that can worsen feelings of panic. Have you ever felt like your anxiety was rapidly spiraling out of control? Breathing was likely at the root of the issue. Anxious thoughts and worries trigger constricted breathing, and the recognition of this restricted breathing tells your body, "Something scary is happening." Round and round the cycle goes. In its extreme form, such anxiety spirals may even turn into full-blown panic attacks.

Belly breathing, or *diaphragmatic breathing*, is a grounding technique that counters this response. By encouraging deep breaths from the diaphragm rather than the chest, belly breathing helps to slow down those anxious sensations—

easing shortness of breath, calming a racing heart, and bringing clarity to the mind. This simple shift in breathing can be incredibly powerful, helping to disrupt the cycle of anxiety before it builds. With deep belly breathing, you create a calming reinforcement loop that helps you gradually calm down over time.

To begin, find a comfortable place to sit or lie down, close your eyes, and let your body start to relax. Take a few moments to settle in, allowing your breathing to slow naturally. There's no rush here—just give yourself permission to unwind.

Now, place a hand on your diaphragm, just beneath your ribs. As you breathe deeply, feel your belly rise with each inhale as the diaphragm moves down. As you exhale, feel your belly fall as the diaphragm relaxes. Focus on keeping the movement centered in your belly, avoiding shallow chest breaths.

Add a gentle visualization. Imagine each breath melting away tension, with every exhale leaving you feeling heavier, your muscles softening. Picture yourself becoming loose and relaxed, like spaghetti, sinking into whatever surface supports you.

It's important to remember that you are never forcing your breath, holding it in or tightening your muscles in any way. One useful visualization is just to imagine that your lungs are bags or balloons, and that air is *passively* filling them up, and then *passively* flowing out again. If it helps, try to imagine that it is the air that is doing the work, and your body is just allowing it to enter, and allowing it to leave again. That's all.

Practice belly breathing for 5-10 minutes daily, even when calm, to build this relaxation response. With regular practice, your body learns to reach this calm state more easily, making it a powerful tool you can rely on whenever anxiety strikes.

LKM

In our most anxious moments, we often speak to ourselves in ways that we wouldn't dream of inflicting on our worst enemy.

It's easy to be kind to others, but when it comes to ourselves, kindness often takes a back seat, doesn't it? *Loving-kindness meditation* (LKM), developed by meditation teacher Michele McDonald and popularized by Jon Kabat-Zinn, offers a powerful way to displace all those anxious feelings of shame, self-hatered, and doubt, and cultivate empathy and warmth..

To start, find a comfortable seat, close your eyes, and settle into your breath. Let your body relax, releasing any tension. Begin by thinking of someone you love deeply—whether a friend, family member, or pet. Allow those good feelings to arise, and practice making them stronger. Really try to conjure up that precise feeling of love, warmth, and acceptance right there in the moment.

Next, gently encapsulate these feelings into phrases like "May you be safe," "May you be happy," "May you be healthy," and "May you live in peace." You can combine this with imagery and visualization as appropriate.

After that, think of someone neutral in your life, like an acquaintance, and offer them the same phrases of kindness. Can you foster the same warm feelings for them as you did for your loved one?

Then bring to mind someone who challenges you—a person who might evoke frustration or annoyance. Can you direct feelings of loving-kindness, acceptance, and grace towards *them*?

This step isn't about resolving conflicts; it's simply about recognizing them with kindness and acceptance. Finally, expand your focus to include everyone—family, neighbors, even strangers—offering each of them wishes for safety, happiness, health, and peace. To finish, direct your loving-kindness towards yourself. Be kind to yourself. See yourself as a loved one would–with acceptance, warmth, and gratitude.

This shift is all about extending the compassion you feel for others back to yourself.

When finished, take a moment to reflect. How did it feel to direct kindness toward yourself? What was it like to send compassion to someone who typically frustrates you? These reflections deepen the experience, helping kindness take root within you. Practiced regularly, LKM can bring serenity, connection, and greater compassion into every corner of your life.

Section 2: Creative Expression and Presence

Doodling

Do you remember doodling as a kid?

As children, doodling came naturally—a playful, unrestricted way to fill the edges of our notebooks with creativity. These days, there are plenty of people trying to formalize the process, selling materials and teaching methods. Though these certainly can't hurt, the truth is that free-form play, creative expression and open-ended exploration are readily available to all of us right now in the moment–and you don't need fancy notebooks, markers, or guides telling you how to do it!

Spontaneous doodling is more than just a pastime; it's a powerful tool that can help us ease psychological tension, boost focus, and find meaning in the everyday. Our minds constantly seek to create coherent narratives from life's experiences, yet sometimes emotions or memories slip through the cracks. Doodling bridges these gaps, tapping into what feels like a mental "time travel machine" that can retrieve forgotten memories or unresolved thoughts, bringing them back into the present.

Doodling, then, is like an unconscious, oblique way of thinking and processing. When we doodle, we put our unconscious mind in charge and let go of expectations and rules. We relax. We stay open-minded and curious. Some days, the process feels like healing and therapy. Other days, it feels like fun and stress relief. Still other days it feels almost like a mystical experience, and a way of touching the as-yet-unknown.

One easy way to start incorporating more doodling into your life is by using a circle doodle template—a sheet with a few blank circles that you can fill however you wish. With this as your canvas, doodles become more than random shapes or quirky designs; they invite meaning to emerge naturally.

Dr. Robert Burns, former director of the Institute for Human Development at the University of Seattle, has studied doodling's power in therapy, viewing it as a window into the unconscious mind. According to Burns, the shapes, patterns, and symbols we create reveal underlying emotions, thoughts, and even tensions we may not fully recognize, akin to an EEG readout reflecting the brain's inner workings.

So, if you're feeling mentally blocked or struggling to focus, try a "doodle break." Set a timer, grab a pen, and let your hand explore freely. Make it meditative or make it playful and silly. See what happens! This simple exercise activates the brain's "unfocus" circuits, giving your "focus" circuits a chance to recharge, often leading to greater clarity and balance.

Calm-Down Mandala Creation

If you're anything like me, you can't help but occasionally doodle a very particular shape: a mandala.

Creating mandalas is a practice that goes far beyond art—it's a journey inward, a tool for cultivating balance, and a pathway to clarity. The word "mandala" itself means "circle," and in many cultures it symbolizes the universe, unity, and connection. Drawing these circular designs allows us to bridge gaps within ourselves, inviting feelings of wholeness, peace, and purpose. Even in times of uncertainty or stress, creating a mandala can serve as a centering experience, helping us realign with what truly matters and find tranquility.

In certain Buddhist traditions, mandala creation is seen as a meditative and holy practice. As you create this mini picture of the universe, you are in a way ordering and centering yourself, finding the right place for your experiences, and connecting yourself and your experiences to the greater whole, internally and externally.

Starting with a mandala template or creating your circle outline is a gentle way to begin. Find a quiet space where you feel comfortable and free from distractions, and gather your art supplies—colored pencils, markers, or even elements from nature like leaves or stones.

Remember that it's not about creating a beautiful outcome; rather, it's the process that matters.

With each line and shape you add, allow yourself to focus not on perfection but on the intention behind each stroke. Use colors, patterns, and symbols that reflect parts of yourself or things that matter to you. Embrace any thoughts, feelings, or memories that arise as you create, treating each design as a moment of self-reflection and presence. Every mandala you create will be unique to the very moment that inspired it. Start with a circle and work inwards, or build your mandala from the center outwards, like a flower. It's up to you/

> This practice is about reconnecting with ourselves and, ultimately, with others. Consider creating mandalas as a family or with friends—sitting side by side in mindful silence, each working on your design or creating one together. It's a beautiful way to bond while inviting peace and connection. Mandala-making encourages us to return to a childlike state of creativity and curiosity, reconnecting with our inner selves.

Gratitude Journal: Three Good Things

As we explored earlier, anxiety and gratitude are like two opposing ends of a continuum.

When our mind is clouded in anxious worry and rumination, it's hard to see the good things around us, as if positivity is hidden behind a thick fog. In this state of mind, even good things that happened to us may be interpreted negatively. We can start to lose our joy in life, and our ability to even *recognize* life's goodness may actually dull over time.

The three good things exercise offers a simple yet transformative way to lift that fog and bring gratitude to the forefront. By writing down three positive moments each day—no matter how big or small—we train our brains to focus on the good, even when life feels challenging. This practice, known as *gratitude journaling*, is backed by research and has been shown to boost positive emotions, improve well-being, and reduce feelings of burnout over time. **Consistently reflecting on these good moments helps create a habit of gratitude, building a more resilient and joyful mindset.**

To get started with the three good things exercise, consider completing prompts like:

"One good thing that happened to me today…"

"Today I had fun when…"

"I'm so glad that…"

These simple phrases make it easier to notice what went well, easing you into a daily gratitude journaling routine. Keep in mind, this is about more than just "going through the motions" or writing down the right words. Try to tap into a genuine *feeling* of gratitude.

If you practice this exercise often enough, you may start to notice things to be grateful for even without prompts, letting gratitude flow naturally. Ultimately, you want to learn to do this without the journal entirely, because you have learned to spot wonderful things in your life as and when they unfold all around you.

Why does this exercise work? Our brains are wired with a negativity bias, meaning we tend to remember negative events more vividly than positive ones. While helpful for survival, this bias can make us overlook the small joys that bring depth and happiness to our lives. The "Three Good Things" exercise actively counters this bias, training us to savor positive emotions like joy, love, and serenity, creating a lasting sense of meaning and fulfillment in the process. Practice it as often as you can.

Stream of Consciousness Writing

Remember the leaves on a stream exercise from earlier on in the book? In that exercise, the leaves were our thoughts, and the stream was our conscious awareness, always flowing, or perhaps even the eternal flow of time passing.

A stream is constant, flowing without pause or hesitation, just like the thoughts that drift through our minds each day. Stream of consciousness journaling captures this natural flow, offering a way to let all those swirling thoughts, questions, worries, and feelings spill onto paper.

While leaves on a stream works primarily because of the concept of *cognitive defusion* (i.e., gaining some psychological distance from our thoughts), the stream of consciousness exercise works more on the concept of *externalization* (i.e. taking your thoughts outside of your mind and putting them outside). Where leaves on a stream is ideal for stress relief and grounding, stream of consciousness writing is more appropriate for processing our thoughts and creative expression.

This unfiltered journaling technique is incredibly accessible—all you need is a pen and paper. With no need for an app or specific notebook, you can start right now, and the benefits can be surprisingly profound.

How does stream of consciousness journaling work? It's simple: Sit down with your paper (or journal if you prefer) and start writing whatever comes to mind. Once the pen tip is on the paper, keep going without stopping. No second-guessing, no editing, no going back to read what you've written—just let your thoughts flow freely. Setting a five-minute timer can provide structure, but if you're in the groove, keep going. Often, you might begin with something simple, like "I don't know what to write," or "I had coffee this morning," but soon, deeper reflections and emotions will start to surface.

This unfiltered approach allows you to explore thoughts without judgment or expectation. Some days, you may uncover an insight or a feeling of relief; other times, it's simply a space to clear out mental clutter—perfect for those overwhelming days when your mind feels crammed with to-do lists. **The aim isn't to be profound, but to free up mental space and to let whatever needs to emerge come through.** Many people find they have no need to actually read what they write!

The best part? No matter what spills onto the page, you'll often find a renewed sense of clarity and calm. This simplicity and sense of release makes stream of consciousness journaling an easy, powerful habit to embrace daily. One small note here: make sure to keep your journal truly private.

Vision Board Creation

Let's take a closer look at vision boards. Though you may have seen plenty of attractive vision boards on social media, these can give unrealistic expectations. **Remember first of all that a vision board is a tool–its purpose is not aesthetic, but therapeutic.**

A vision board is more than a collection of images; it's a psychological tool that can enhance mental health and provide clarity. Visualization can play a powerful role in shaping our beliefs about what's possible. By actively envisioning positive outcomes, we're more likely to feel motivated, resilient, and focused, especially during challenging times.

Creating and viewing a vision board provides a sense of purpose and direction, reinforcing the goals we care about most and helping counter the effects of anxiety and stress. You create a tangible focal point to direct your awareness towards. Studies have shown that engaging in creative activities like making a vision board can relieve symptoms of depression, lower stress, and encourage emotional processing by giving space for reflection and imagination. Once the vision board is made, you renew your commitment to your goals every time you look at it and remind yourself of your intentions. This daily practice alone can be incredibly centering and motivational.

To create a vision board, first, clarify your goals. Take time to think about what matters to you, whether it's career aspirations, personal growth, strengthened relationships, or improved well-being.

Once you have an idea, gather materials like magazines, photos, quotes, or even personal items such as postcards or drawings. Select visuals that resonate with your goals, focusing on images and words that inspire or represent who you want to become.

Then, arrange these elements thoughtfully on your board, placing core goals at the center or in prominent spots. Let this process be intentional—there's no rush. Enjoy putting together your aspirations in a way that's visually inspiring and meaningful.

When your board is finished, display it somewhere you'll see it daily, like next to your bed or near your desk.

By integrating this vision into your routine, your board becomes a daily source of motivation, a reminder of what you're working toward, and a mental health booster that keeps you grounded and inspired while you pursue your goals.

Self-Care Collage

These days, practices like vision board creation and visualization are gaining more and more popularity. When you feel like you've been stuck in your head too long, it can be great to create something practical and to express yourself through the medium of pictures instead.

Creating a self-care collage is a refreshingly practical way to design a personal self-care plan. Think of it as building a visual blueprint for the moments you need most. It's not just about pinning up things you like; it's about understanding what genuinely helps you decompress, recharge, and feel more balanced. Then, you get to work towards manifesting that vision in pictorial form.

To get started, gather some materials: magazines, scissors, blank paper, and glue. As you pull together images, words, or even colors that feel like "you," start homing in on a couple of core self-care needs, such as deep breathing and sensory awareness—two essentials for any solid self-care plan.

For example, deep breathing can be considered a foundational tool for your self-care. Consider when and where you'd want to incorporate deep breaths into your routine. Maybe it's every morning before you jump out of bed, or right before you face that challenging midweek class or meeting. Grab visuals that remind you to pause and breathe—images of calm skies, peaceful landscapes, or simple symbols that prompt you to reset.

Remember the body scan coloring exercise? Why not incorporate your specific colors, shapes, and symbols into your collage? Similarly, you might like to print out particularly impactful affirmations, words, or quotes to quickly remind you of what you're trying to achieve.

Another example is *sensory self-care.* This is about tuning into what works for each of your senses. Reflect on what feels overwhelming, calming, or right regarding sound, touch, taste, sight, and smell. Maybe you need complete quiet after a busy day or find that the smell of fresh coffee grounds centers you. Let your collage represent these preferences with images or textures that fit. Depending on how creative you want to be, you can even play around with very tactile elements, like pieces of material, dried flowers, foil, stickers, photographs, ribbons, or pieces of ephemera that jog particular memories.

When you're done, put your collage somewhere that you'll see it regularly. This isn't just about creating something beautiful (indeed, it might not be beautiful at all!); it's **a visual tool for**

reconnecting with yourself and prioritizing your well-being.

Poetry for Relaxation

One thing I especially like to include on vision boards is poetry. The right words can be amazingly evocative–and that's whether the words are your own or someone else's.

Writing poetry offers a unique way for you to release and process complex emotions, creating a safe and expressive space to confront complicated feelings.. Through poetry, writers can take time to observe, label, and honestly express what's going on within, allowing them to acknowledge emotions and release thoughts they may have unknowingly suppressed. This is the practice of externalization and defusion again.

Poetry doesn't just help with releasing emotions; it also supports the growth of self-confidence and self-worth. For those who have experienced trauma or hardship, rebuilding self-esteem can be a difficult journey.

You can begin to separate the truth from anxious self-beliefs by writing and sharing poetry. Writing allows one's voice to take center stage, transforming a quiet, internal experience into something that can be shared. This process is empowering for many people, giving them the courage to reclaim their story and inspire others to do the same. Something magical happens when you put your feelings down in black and white.

To begin writing poetry for relaxation, one simple exercise involves using a word bank focused on mental health or emotional themes. Start by jotting down a few feeling words, images, or ideas that immediately pop into your mind. You could even include little sketches or doodles; the point, at first, is just to brainstorm freely.

Next, use these words as prompts to create poetry, crafting verses that reflect your experiences and insights. It doesn't have to rhyme, and it doesn't have to be long. You don't have to show your work to anyone. Remember, the goal is not the finished product, but the process you access along the way.

Emotions Wheel Exercise

How emotionally literate are you?

Do you know what you're feeling when you're feeling it?

For those of us who struggle with anxiety, life can sometimes feel dominated by fear and apprehensiveness. This narrow focus can rob us of a deeper understanding of all the other shades of emotions we feel throughout life.

The following exercise is inspired by a technique used in art therapy and is designed to help you explore and express your emotions. The goal is to help you gain more emotional fluency and higher self-awareness throughout the process.

Emotions are complex, sometimes overwhelming forces that shape our experiences, yet understanding them can feel elusive. The emotions wheel exercise offers a creative and non-judgmental way to explore these emotions, helping you capture and interpret each feeling visually. By pairing emotions with colors or images that resonate with how you experience them, this exercise becomes a powerful tool for self-reflection and emotional clarity.

To begin, draw a big circle on an average-sized piece of paper. Then, divide the circle into quarters, and divide those again to yield eight equal segments, a little like a pizza. Each segment will be devoted to exploring and expressing a specific emotion, for example:

Anger

Surprise

Joy

Disgust

Fear

Sadness

Confusion

Shame

You can choose the emotions that work best for you. Next, choose a color that best captures the feeling each one brings up for you. For example, maybe anger feels like a vibrant red, while eagerness might be a bright yellow. If any images or symbols come to mind, include those too—anger might be a jagged line, or fear could be a dark cloud. Essentially, you are doodling. If you want to take things further, you could even use collage techniques to more fully complete each segment.

After filling in each section, take a moment to reflect on why you chose each color or image. What about that shade or symbol aligns with how you feel when experiencing that particular emotion? When last did you feel this emotion? Which emotion do you experience most often? Least often? This step encourages deeper thought about your emotional responses, helping you connect with what each feeling truly means to you.

The emotions wheel exercise invites you to express your emotions freely and without judgment. This is a big part of learning to accept and overcome the default "fear" setting that many anxiety-sufferers experience. It also helps develop an understanding of where your anxiety is coming from; it may not even be from fear, but rather from sadness, anger, or confusion. By assigning colors and images, you can observe your emotions with greater objectivity, transforming your feelings into insights rather than reactive states. This process supports a mindful and accepting approach to emotions, bringing you closer to a balanced understanding of your inner landscape.

Gratitude Jar

This tip is a little like a combination of a gratitude journal and the mindfulness bingo card. A jar can hold more than just objects—it can be a vessel for capturing moments of joy, gratitude, and reflection. Keeping a gratitude jar is a powerful yet simple practice that encourages you to pause each day and reconnect with the small things that bring happiness, grounding you in the positive. In our busy lives, it's easy to let these moments slip by unnoticed, but a gratitude jar helps keep them alive.

To begin, find a clear jar or container and place it somewhere visible, like on your desk or bedside table, as a gentle reminder to take a moment for gratitude. Gather slips of paper, a pen, and any decorative touches you like—stickers, markers, or ribbons can make it personal. Each day, or whenever you feel inspired, jot down three things you're grateful for. They don't have to be monumental; perhaps it's "enjoying a warm cup of tea," or "having a meaningful conversation with a friend." If you're unsure where to start, use prompts like "Today, I felt grateful for...," or "I appreciated...."

Drop each note into your jar, watching it slowly fill with these positive reflections. You can make a little ritual where, for example, you write 1–3 things down on a piece of paper every morning or evening. Use Post-it notes or colored strips of paper. Some people like to include little objects that visually remind them of everything they have to be grateful for: a pretty stone picked up on a walk, a coin that symbolizes a raise or a financial windfall, a tiny scrap of fabric from a favorite garment–you get the idea.

Over time, you'll curate a collection of reminders to look back on whenever you need a lift. The next time you feel full of fears and grumbles and complaints, glance at your jar and see just how many separate incidents of abundance and good fortune you've actually experienced. It's like a very practical way to count your blessings!

This simple habit has a ripple effect on well-being. Building gratitude into your day rewires your mind to notice the positive, even on tough days. As the jar fills, it becomes a powerful visual reminder of all the good in your life, helping you feel grounded, connected, and resilient when you need it most. Notice the good in your life and *keep* it. Store it up. Teach yourself that these things are accumulating, slowly but surely, day after day.

Life Story

When you are an anxious overthinker, constant nervous energy and negative self-talk can have a fracturing effect on your reality. It can feel like the chaos is breaking everything into splinters. It can be hard to look beyond the current worry or agitation that is filling your awareness in the present moment.

One way to zoom out of this anxious tunnel vision is to learn to consciously remind yourself of the bigger picture.

Your life so far is a story rich with experiences, lessons, and dreams yet to be realized. It is so, so much more than the challenges that are bothering you today, or the snags and fears that have currently caught your attention.

The life story exercise invites you to explore this journey in three parts: past, present, and future. Rooted in positive psychology and narrative therapy, this approach helps you connect with your strengths, clarify your purpose, and create a vision for what lies ahead.

Begin with the past. Reflect on key moments that have shaped who you are today—the challenges you've faced, the achievements that brought joy, and even the setbacks that taught you resilience. Writing about these experiences can reveal hidden strengths like courage, adaptability, and self-compassion, offering a fresh perspective on how you've grown. Of course, you can incorporate any other creative elements you like, such as sketching, painting, poetry, and so on.

Next, focus on the present. Consider your current goals, values, and strengths, grounding yourself in what supports your well-being and fulfillment right now. This step serves as a reminder that you're already equipped with resources that foster growth and resilience.

Finally, turn to the future. Imagine your ideal life and the goals you wish to pursue. Picture the person you aspire to become and identify the steps you must take to reach that vision. Aligning your future aspirations with your strengths empowers you to move forward with confidence and purpose.

You don't need to spend hours crafting a perfectly accurate and comprehensive historical account–ten minutes is enough to remind yourself that there is life beyond whatever is bothering you in the here and now. You are more than your emotions, and your experiences don't define you. Remember that your story is not over–it continues into the future.

The life story exercise is more than a reflection; it's a meaningful guide that honors your past, embraces your present, and inspires your future. Through this exercise, you create a personal narrative that celebrates your journey, reinforces your purpose, and propels you forward with clarity and intention. The life story allows you to broaden (and relax) your view.

The Tree of Life

Have you ever considered a tree a symbol of your life journey? We've mentioned trees and leaves quite a few times so far in this book, and there's a reason for that. Trees are powerful, primal symbols that speak very deeply to our unconscious minds. The tree of life exercise uses the potent image of a tree to help you explore your past, celebrate your present, and envision your future.

Underneath it all we understand the symbolism: it's about growth and continuity.

To begin, draw a simple tree with essential parts—roots, trunk, branches, leaves, and perhaps a few optional elements. Remember, the goal is reflection, not artistry, so keep it as simple as you'd like. You don't have to show anyone your work, and you can destroy the finished piece when you're done.

The roots and the soil represent your past, capturing the people, places, and events that have shaped you. Here, reflect on the foundational experiences and influences that ground you today. The grass or ground symbolizes your present, a space for noting the routines, activities, or passions that bring you energy and joy. The trunk is where you identify your core strengths, values, and defining traits—the qualities that give you resilience and direction.

Now, look to the branches to map out your dreams and aspirations. Write down both short- and long-term goals, from personal ambitions to hopes for your community or the world. You might like to pay attention to where the trunk branches off. Do you wish to memorialize certain big events or decisions that shaped your path in life? You can use each branch to represent a different goal, or a different part of yourself–or a mix of all these.

On the leaves, you may include the people and pets who support or inspire you—those who make your life richer. The fruits could symbolize the gifts and lessons you've received from others, whether it's wisdom, kindness, or any meaningful legacy they've passed on.

Optional elements add depth: flowers for the legacy you wish to leave, clouds for obstacles, a compost bin for past challenges, and a bird for sources of joy. It's your tree, and you get to decide what it looks like! When complete, your tree of life becomes a visual narrative of your journey, emphasizing your strengths and dreams—a source of inspiration to keep you grounded and connected to your path.

One thing you may discover is that this exercise reveals a lot more than you expected. It's only when you take the time to pull all your disparate life experiences into a single image, on one page, that you can start to really grasp the bigger picture. You may start to see patterns in where your anxiety and core beliefs have come from, and how they are manifesting today. You may surprise yourself at the sudden connections you make, or bigger, overarching themes you uncover. Whatever the case, it's all part of the tree–it's all you.

Inside Out/Outside In

Have you ever peeled an orange and noticed the difference between the tough outer rind and the delicate fruit inside? The inside out/outside in self-portrait exercise takes a similar approach, inviting you to explore the layers of yourself—the parts you keep hidden and the face you show to the world.

To begin, draw or find a simple silhouette to use as the foundation of your portrait. The most ideal shape to use is a simple outline of a neck and shoulders. One idea is to tape a blank sheet of paper on the wall and literally trace your shadow to yield a silhouette. You'll get the same result, however, by just sketching a simple outline of a person in portrait. This outline represents your self-portrait, ready for both your inner world and outer expression to come to life. The line you've drawn represents the boundary, the interface, between the inside and the outside.

As you fill in the inside of your silhouette, focus on your core qualities. What defines you at your deepest level? If you were to be opened up (on a symbolic level, of course!) what would people find inside? What is something that people don't know about you, or perhaps something that you conceal? Think of the dreams, emotions, and truths that often stay beneath the surface. How might you represent those in drawings, sketches, and symbols? This is where you capture the inner layers that shape you, beyond any roles or labels you may hold.

For example, you might draw a very big heart that nevertheless has a hole in it, or a little whirlwind to represent your anxiety, or a tiny version of a loved one with lightning bolts emanating from their mouths.

Next, on the outside of the silhouette, reflect on how you think others see you. What do people tend to notice about you? Consider the impressions friends, family, or society may have, including any labels or assumptions. Use words, symbols, or images to illustrate this external self, the version others are most familiar with.

For example, you might draw a series of daggers coming towards you, or write out words and phrases people have used to label you, perhaps each in a different color. You may also pay some attention to the line itself. Is it very solid? Permeable? Unclear?

When you're done, step back and examine the balance or contrast between your inner truth and outer expression. Notice how these two perspectives interact and reflect on what they reveal about your identity. This exercise is a powerful reminder that both sides—the visible and hidden—are vital parts of you, encouraging self-acceptance and a richer understanding of who you truly are.

Turning Anxiety to Calm

Whether you're a professional artist or someone who simply likes sketching and doodling, there is something truly thrilling about sitting before the blank page. What follows is a simple yet powerful meditation exercise that requires just two things: a bank sheet of paper, and your mind (whatever state it happens to be in!).

A sheet of paper might seem pretty ordinary, but in the turning anxiety into calm exercise, it becomes a powerful tool for transformation.

Here, we will work with *externalization* again, and take part in a very literal process of **transforming whatever is inside our minds into something *out there* in the world**. For many artists, this process is at the very heart of creation.

Imagine taking all those swirling thoughts and feelings of overwhelm in your mind and turning them into a visual reminder of peace. This exercise invites you to not just face your anxiety, but to interact with it, ultimately transforming it into something grounding and beautiful. It is most fundamentally a *productive* act–we do something with our thoughts and feelings, and we make something of them. In the process, we process! In this exercise, the first medium we use will not be crayon or paint or ink, but our own hands and fingers.

To begin, grab a blank piece of paper and take a quick mental check-in. Rate your current anxiety level on a scale from 1 to 10, and jot that number down elsewhere as your starting point. Now, take a deep breath, and visualize each worry, every anxious thought, traveling down your arm, through your fingers, and into the paper. Hold it tightly, squeeze it, crumple it—imagine channeling all of that energy directly into this paper ball. Take your time with this step–really imagine your mental and emotional energy flowing out of you.

When you feel ready, carefully unfold and flatten the paper. Now, with markers or colored pencils, let the creases and lines from crumpling become your canvas. Use those lines as a guide, filling in shapes, tracing patterns, or adding colors that feel calming. What starts out as shattered, spidery shapes becomes a stained-glass window or a tree. Each little crumple is a new shape, a new little corner of possibility. This part of the exercise is about transformation—taking the remnants of tension and creating art that embodies calmness. When your feelings are externalized this way, you are empowered to work on them. You can slow down. You can re-imagine. You can give shape and form.

Finally, take another moment to check in with yourself. Rate your anxiety once more and notice any shifts. What is your number now?

This exercise serves as a reminder that, with intention, we can transform our inner state. What feels overwhelming today can become a foundation for calm and creativity, offering you a way to reshape stress into something soothing and empowering.

Affirmation Art

Some people resonate naturally with images, colors, and shapes. For others, it's words that hold the most power. For many people, it's a blend of the two that speaks most directly to their hearts. This is what we'll focus on with this activity.

Creating art that utilizes positive affirmations is more than just an artistic activity—it's a powerful tool to foster self-acceptance, resilience, and a positive outlook. When we focus on affirmations, we're crafting mindful statements that reinforce our strengths and uplift our spirits.

This practice is especially helpful when life's challenges seem to cloud our perspective. Through affirmations, we can actively choose thoughts that empower us. Words like "I am enough," or "I am in charge of how I feel," can be transformative, helping us to develop a healthier self-image and an appreciation for our unique journey.

Start by gathering a piece of paper, pastels or markers, and watercolors. Select an object that feels meaningful—perhaps a flower, a favorite memento, or something ordinary like a rock from your garden. Trace its outline repeatedly on your paper in different colors, creating overlapping shapes and patterns. Once you've traced your object, use watercolors to fill in each area, embracing any flow or interaction between the colors. This is not dissimilar from the process you followed in the previous exercise.

After the paint dries, add affirmations directly onto your artwork. You could write them with a bold marker, use cut-out words, or even stamp them on. Choose affirmations that speak to where you are in life or ones that address specific challenges. Some ideas include: "My thoughts are filled with positivity," "I am grateful for my journey," or "I trust myself to overcome obstacles."

When you see these affirmations alongside your art, you create a visual reminder of your growth and potential. **Each time you engage with this artwork, you reinforce positive beliefs, helping to transform fleeting affirmations into sustained thoughts**. A great idea is to display your artwork somewhere you can see it every day (perhaps next to your bed, on the fridge, or near your work desk) and take a moment whenever you glimpse it to repeat the affirmations in your own mind. Another interesting idea is to make your artwork progressive; in other words, keep adding to it over time. What you will be creating is not just a visual reminder, but a way to track and monitor your own development over time.

Picture of Me

People who suffer from anxiety can often start to feel like their worry and overthinking is all that defines them, is all that they are as people. It can begin to seem like anxiety is a kind of cage in which we are trapped, and the only identity we have is a prisoner of that cage. But it's not true!

You are so much more than the noise in your brain, and you have a purpose and role outside of whatever "traffic" is running around in your mind. What's more, you don't have to be completely healed or cured of your anxiety forever in order to claim and own these other identities. You can occasionally struggle with stress and overthinking without losing your identity as a good friend, say, or as a mother, sister, artist, professional, and so on. This exercise is about reminding you that, even though it doesn't always feel like it, you are bigger than your anxiety.

In your lifetime, you see many photos of yourself—each capturing a moment, a mood, a piece of who you are. But rarely do these snapshots capture the *full* story of your identity. The pictures of me: identity exploration exercise offers a way to dive deeper, helping you visually explore the many roles, traits, and experiences that make you uniquely you. This is a chance to reflect on the parts of yourself that often go unnoticed or unexpressed.

Start by listing several aspects of your identity that are meaningful to you. These might include roles like being a parent, friend, or mentor; traits such as resilience, humor, or empathy; or experiences that have shaped you, like being a survivor or living with a chronic illness. You may also include visions, goals, and values you hold.

Next, for each part of your identity, create a mini artwork—either a drawing or a collage—that represents it. Use images, symbols, or objects that resonate with you. If nature is a core part of your identity, you might draw mountains or trees; if kindness is essential to you, symbols of hands or hearts might feel fitting. Collage materials like magazines and cut-outs can add texture and depth if you prefer working with found images.

Once you've completed each piece, take a moment to reflect. Ask yourself: Which part of your identity feels most authentic? What values are associated with each role or trait? Are there pieces of your identity that you tend to keep private, and others you openly express? You may spontaneously discover that there is something about your identity that you'd like to nurture, grow, or share more widely.

This exercise provides a powerful pathway to self-understanding, revealing how each part of your identity connects with your values, emotions, and how you engage with the world. Anxiety may be a part of that picture, but it's never the *whole* picture.

Section 3: Practical Strategies for Life Management

Daily Time Management

Imagine someone who gets to bed late one evening because they watched TV for longer than they planned. Because they go to bed late, they oversleep the next morning. They don't have enough time to eat breakfast, and in the mad morning rush they forget a few things at home, which leads to more chaos later in the day.

Just before lunch, they discover that they've double-booked their midday appointment because they didn't write anything down, then they turn up in error to a meeting that was actually cancelled last week, effectively wasting that hour. By the time they get home that evening, they're frazzled and exhausted, just to discover that they have forgotten what day it is–their spouse's birthday. They're late to the restaurant and lose their booking.

Now, before bed this person notices their extremely anxious and strung-out mood, and says to themselves, "My life's a mess, I need some stress-management or something." But they're wrong. They don't need stress management, but *time* management.

Time management is more than just fitting tasks into a schedule—it's about bringing a sense of control and calm into daily life. It's one of our most powerful tools to reduce and moderate the everyday stresses and anxieties of life. With only 24 hours in a day, managing time well helps ensure that those hours serve our goals, well-being, and relationships.

Rather than feeling overwhelmed by endless to-dos, good time management allows you to prioritize what truly matters, reducing the scramble and creating room for relaxation, growth, and joy. It's about giving yourself *less* to do and worry about.

Effective time management can transform a day, offering benefits that go beyond productivity. It reduces stress by allowing you to prepare for tasks in advance, rather than cramming them into the last minute. This proactive approach builds confidence, improves the quality of your work, and lessens the anxiety that comes from feeling rushed. It also creates a sense of balance, giving you the freedom to enjoy the present instead of feeling like you're constantly catching up.

To get a clear picture of how you spend your day, start by creating a simple breakdown of your activities. Draw a big circle on a piece of paper, then divide it into sections that represent each hour – like a pie chart. Fill in the tasks or activities that make up your day, from essentials like sleep, work, and meals to personal time, family obligations, or hobbies. Include any recurring tasks, even the small ones like commuting or preparing meals.

Once your daily layout is complete, review it to see where your hours are going. Look for any areas where time could be reallocated to support your well-being, such as adding a relaxation break or reducing time spent on distractions. Deliberately schedule in time for the things you know are important, and set reminders and alarms for yourself. When you start taking ownership of your time, you may suddenly find that there is more of it at your disposal!

(GROW) Goal-Setting Worksheet

Having no goals can make you feel lost, as though you're drifting without direction. Many people may find themselves ruminating and overthinking about "nothing," but on closer inspection, their fears have a basis in reality. They may feel that they should be doing something... but they aren't. If you've ever felt this way, it may be a sign that you are lacking direction, purpose, and focus around a meaningful goal.

The GROW goal-setting model serves as a compass for your personal and professional journey, steering you toward meaningful achievements. Created in the 1980s by coaches

Graham Alexander, Alan Fine, and Sir John Whitmore, this framework revolves around four essential pillars: Goals, reality, options, and way forward.

Goals: Start with clarity. Reflect on what you truly want to achieve and how it aligns with your core values. Ask yourself, "What do I want to create in my life?" When your goals resonate deeply, they ignite the passion that fuels your journey. Goals can be big or small, abstract or concrete, short-term or long-term.

Reality: Next, assess your current situation. Where do you stand in relation to your goals? Honest reflection helps identify obstacles and strengths. Consider questions like, "What barriers am I facing?" to illuminate your path ahead. Consider the strengths and opportunities that exist to help you achieve your goal, as well as limitations and weaknesses that could undermine it. Be realistic without being judgmental.

Options: With your goals and reality in mind, explore the possibilities. What options are available to you? Embrace creativity by asking questions like, "What different routes can I take?" and "Who can support me?" This exploration opens your mind to various strategies and resources. Ask for help, learn more, seek a mentor, enroll in a course, or experiment to gather more data.

Way Forward: Finally, devise a plan of action. What steps will you take to turn your dreams into reality? Reflect on questions like, "What is my first step?" and "How will I hold myself accountable?" This commitment transforms aspirations into actionable steps, guiding you toward success. One of the best ways to lower anxiety about the path ahead is to break everything down into small steps. Just focus on the steps you need to take today.

By incorporating these guiding questions into the GROW model, you create a clear path for achieving your goals. Whether in your personal life, career, or relationships, the GROW model helps you connect with your vision and take actionable steps to bring it to fruition. If you find yourself feeling anxious in this area, remind yourself of the goal, the path ahead and the options available to you. Be patient and rest in that purpose.

Eisenhower Matrix for Prioritization

There are a million things to do every day, right?

It seems like everyone wants a piece of you, and your attention is being pulled in dozens of different directions. Bills, chores, errands, emails, text messages, notifications, deadlines, events... how on earth are you supposed to decide what to focus on? Isn't it all important?

The answer is no. Only *some* of it is important. What's more, not everything is urgent. You only have so much time and attention; trying to do everything will only lead to anxiety, stress, worry, and overwhelm.

What if the hack to mastering productivity and beating stress lies in a simple matrix that acknowledges both the relative importance and the urgency of every possible task you could encounter?

The *Eisenhower Matrix*, a powerful organizational tool created by Dwight D. Eisenhower, offers just that. By helping you distinguish between urgent and important tasks, this matrix streamlines your decision-making, planning, and prioritizing, allowing you to manage your time more effectively.

The activity involves categorizing tasks into four distinct quadrants based on their urgency and importance:

Quadrant I: Urgent & Important Tasks

These are tasks that need immediate attention and are critical to your goals, such as deadlines or emergencies. Addressing them first ensures you stay on top of high-stakes responsibilities. For example, a big fine that will result in legal action if not paid in a week, or a family member's unexpected death and funeral.

Quadrant II: Not Urgent & Important Tasks

Here, you'll list tasks that are essential for long-term success, but don't require immediate action. Planning, self-care, and skill development fall here—imperative for steady progress without the pressure of urgency. An example for this quadrant would be your weekly workouts, going to a lecture, or working on a submission for a competition you are hoping to win in two months' time.

Quadrant III: Urgent & Not Important Tasks

In this quadrant, you'll identify tasks that feel urgent but don't significantly impact your goals, like interruptions or non-essential requests. These can often be delegated or minimized. A classic example is junk mail arriving in your inbox that announces itself as "URGENT!" While it's true that their special 90% off sale on air mattresses will only last this weekend, that fact is utterly unimportant to you.

Quadrant IV: Not Urgent & Not Important Tasks

This quadrant contains distractions that take up time without contributing to your objectives, such as excessive social media scrolling or mindless TV watching. You probably don't need an example here, as you can easily imagine which parts of your own day eat up time in this way. Reducing these activities frees up time and energy for what truly matters.

Using the Eisenhower Matrix brings clarity to your priorities, highlighting where to focus your energy. **Not only will you be more organized, but you'll be more focused, which invariably makes you less anxious and stressed.** This simple tool empowers you to manage your time effectively, reducing stress and boosting productivity in every area of life.

Generating Alternative Solutions and Better Decision Making

The word "ruminate" comes from the Latin root that means "to chew." Ruminants are those animals that chew the cud, and when we ruminate, this is exactly what we're doing: we're chewing over the same old ideas, again and again. Thinking is a wonderful thing; *over*thinking, however, is not. Sometimes, the trouble is that we are allowing useless and unproductive *rumination* to get in the way of genuine, helpful *thinking*.

Rumination may feel like problem solving, but it isn't. How can you tell the difference?

Rumination never results in action or resolution, whereas healthy problem solving always pushes into *action*. Problem solving results in change.

When you're faced with a challenge, gathering insights from others can be incredibly beneficial, and can help you get out of your head and into useful action. This activity, generating alternative solutions and better decision making, invites you to lay out your situation and the obstacles standing in your way. Don't hesitate to share the details—this is your chance to get a fresh perspective.

First, think about the various solutions that could address your problem. Write down five alternative solutions that come to mind and evaluate each one. Consider these key questions: Will it work? Can I realistically carry it out? What effects will this have on me personally-both positive and negative? What are the social implications? How will these solutions impact my relationships or community?

As you fill out this information, you'll not only clarify your options, but also gain deeper insights into the potential outcomes of each choice. Remember, the goal is not just to find a quick fix, but to reflect on how each solution aligns with your core values and long-term goals. Try to keep judgment out of the process and stay open-minded. Once you've gone through this process, identify the solution that resonates the most with you and feels achievable. It may not be a particularly likeable solution, but satisfy yourself that it is the best path given your various options. The best way to move on from anxiously thinking about a decision or problem is to take inspired action.

Finally, if you feel comfortable, share your decision-making process with someone else. Getting feedback can further refine your thoughts and boost your confidence in moving forward. It can remind you that you always have the power to be proactive about your life, and what happens in it.

Embrace rumination as an opportunity to empower yourself to take control of your choices and create a path that leads to personal growth and fulfillment. After all, every decision shapes your journey, and by actively engaging in this process, you're investing in your future.

Boundary-Setting Worksheet

For some of us, stress and anxiety arise not because of poor time management, ill-defined goals, or a lack of strategy when it comes to making decisions. Instead, stress may come from the fact that our boundaries are not as healthy as they could be.

Setting boundaries is essential for maintaining healthy relationships and protecting your well-being. *Boundaries,* in this context, are the limits and rules we establish for ourselves, allowing us to say "no" when needed while still fostering intimacy and connection with others. Our boundaries and limits protect our finite resources–our time, energy, attention, even things like material possessions or money. This activity, setting boundaries, is designed to help you identify and communicate your boundaries more effectively.

Start by reflecting on your personal values, as these will guide the boundaries you set. Think about what matters most to you in life, as well as the things you don't have any time or energy for whatsoever. Next, consider the areas of life right now that are most stress-filled for you, and think about whether your boundaries are functioning well in this area. For example, is someone encroaching on your time, your privacy, or your sense of self-esteem?

Next, think about ways you might tighten up these boundaries by communicating more assertively. For example, you might say, "I'm not comfortable with this," or "This doesn't work for me." Practice responding to various scenarios by considering the language you'd use to establish your boundaries in a polite, yet firm way.

In addition to verbal communication, focus on your body language. Use confident posture, maintain eye contact, and speak in a steady tone. Remember to be respectful, avoiding aggressive language while still being firm about your needs.

Remember that people can and will press on boundaries–that doesn't mean that you aren't entitled to have them, or that you are doing anything wrong by asserting them! Stay firm. Planning ahead for difficult discussions can also help you feel more confident in asserting your boundaries.

If boundary-setting is difficult, think carefully about the language you are using. Try not to apologize for stating needs or limits. Don't soften or hedge your language, avoid passive-aggression, and plainly and clearly repeat yourself if necessary–no excuses or justifications needed.

Finally, consider the balance of give-and-take in relationships. While it's important to stand by your boundaries, listening to others and being open to compromise can strengthen your connections. Relationships are never super neat and tidy, and sometimes you will need to put others first. If you're ever unsure, remember that there's nothing wrong with buying time by saying something like, "I'm not sure. Can I come back to you with an answer later?"

Develop a Self-Care Plan

Stress and anxiety are a little like a check engine light on a car dashboard. They tell us that, even though the car may still be running, something is not right and requires attention. If you are routinely feeling overwhelmed, stressed, and anxious, this may be a warning light telling you that a little TLC is needed somewhere in your life.

Practicing self-care is crucial for maintaining overall well-being, especially when navigating life's challenges or supporting someone else with their own challenges. Engaging in a consistent self-care routine can transform your mental landscape, alleviating anxiety and depression while reducing stress and enhancing happiness. Self-care is like getting regular car maintenance; keeping the tires pumped up, oil changed, and the gas tank full will help prevent tons of complications down the road.

The evidence is clear: a national survey revealed that 64% of Americans reported improved self-confidence, 67% noted increased productivity, and 71% experienced greater happiness as a result of self-care practices. Moreover, prioritizing self-care contributes to better physical health, lowering the risk of conditions like heart disease, stroke, and cancer.

If you were to rate our ability to *consistently* care for yourself, on a scale of 1 to 10, how would rate yourself? Try to be honest about your current self-care status right now.

Rate your consistency with the following self-care habits on a scale from 1 to 5, where 5 indicates that you frequently engage in the habit, and 1 means it never occurred to you:

Sleep

Healthy diet

Time for rest and relaxation

Time in nature

Socializing with friends and family

Spiritual life

Creative expression

Fun and entertainment

Personal development

Health care

Mindfulness

Relationships

Grooming

Exercise

Next, identify three areas that could use the most attention right now. Let's say, those that score below 3. What small things can you do right now, today, to take a step towards improving your self-care in that area? It could be something as simple as taking a few breaks at work, treating yourself to an herbal tea, or calling up a friend. Reflect on obstacles that might hinder your self-care efforts and brainstorm possible solutions.

After completing this assessment, you can use the insights gained to develop a personalized, long-term self-care plan. Commit to making those small changes more permanent; for example, aim to get 7 hours sleep tonight, then try to get three good nights of sleep in a row, then push that to a week, and so on until the habit is more embedded in your routine.

By committing to new self-care practices, you'll pave the way for a more balanced and fulfilling life. Remember, prioritizing your well-being is not just an act of kindness toward yourself; it's a powerful foundation for resilience and happiness. Take it slow and be patient–the most impactful thing you can do is make a tiny change, but keep it up for the rest of your life!

Time Blocking Activity

Have you ever felt like you've spent an entire day busily rushing from one task to the other, and yet somehow at the end of the day it seems like you've accomplished barely anything? If so, you may appreciate a simple time management technique called blocking.

Time blocking is your beacon, like a lighthouse in the chaos of a busy week, a tool to help you cut through the noise and regain your focus. When you glance at the days ahead and feel that familiar wave of overwhelm, remember: Breaking your tasks into manageable chunks can change everything. This approach empowers you to take the reins of your time, making it easier to zero in on what truly matters.

The beauty of time blocking lies in its straightforwardness. Rather than spreading your attention thin over endless hours, you carve out specific slots—usually an hour or less—for each task. Once you finish a block, take a moment to breathe. Let your mind reset before diving into the next project. This rhythm not only helps you avoid burnout, but also allows you to tackle your work with renewed energy and a fresh perspective.

As you start this journey, set realistic expectations. Even if you commit just 10 to 15 minutes to a task, that's a win. Experiment with time intervals that feel right for you, and don't shy away from establishing boundaries in your space. Limit distractions, create an environment conducive to focus, and remember to incorporate breaks into your schedule. Those moments of rest are just as vital as the work itself.

To get started with time blocking, find or create a simple page broken down into hour and half-hour slots, like those you often see in work diaries. You'll need one per day. Now, plan ahead by scheduling all the tasks you have to do, each with a defined beginning and ending. Use timers to let you know when to switch tasks, remembering to schedule in regular breaks.

This process may seem quite obvious, but the truth is that it's easy to lose focus throughout the day and drift off task. A good idea is to clump similar tasks together so that you reduce the "attentional cost" of task-switching. This will allow you to engage in deep work for longer periods, and, counterintuitively, this feels far less stressful and overwhelming. If possible, try to focus on a just one main task a day, so that you stay "in the zone."

Procrastination Worksheet

Procrastination, that nagging voice telling you to put things off until tomorrow, often feels like an insurmountable wall blocking your path to success.. The more you procrastinate, the more anxious you feel, but the more anxious you feel, the more you procrastinate! To combat this pervasive issue, try a three-part activity designed to help you break free from avoidance and step into a calmer, more fulfilling life.

We begin with the procrastination checklist, a reflective tool that invites you to assess how procrastination impacts various aspects of your life: work, health, relationships, and personal development. It has been adapted from *Procrastination: Why You Do It, What to Do About It (Burka & Yuen, 1983).*

Mark areas where procrastination seems to affect you the most. Are deadlines slipping away? Are you neglecting self-care or vital relationships? Recognizing these patterns is crucial, as it marks the first step toward reclaiming control over your time and energy.

ACADEMICS

❏ Going to class on time

❏ Completing readings

❏ Completing assignments

❏ Preparing for exams

❏ Writing papers

❏ Starting/finishing long-term projects

❏ Setting short-term goals

❏ Setting long-term goals

❏ Finding/organizing a study group

❏ Making tutoring/coaching appointments

❏ Communicating with instructors

- ❏ Making an advising appointment
- ❏ Registering for next semester
- ❏ Selecting a major and/or minor
- ❏ Utilizing campus resources
- ❏ Submitting financial aid forms (FAFSA, scholarship applications, etc.)
- ❏ Finding a job

- ❏ Other: _____

PERSONAL WELLNESS/MAINTENANCE
- ❏ Eating
- ❏ Exercising
- ❏ Sleeping
- ❏ Maintaining personal hygiene
- ❏ Fulfilling financial responsibilities
- ❏ Paying bills
- ❏ Creating a budget

❏ Sticking to a budget
❏ Doing chores
❏ Laundry
❏ Cleaning/dishes
❏ Grocery shopping
❏ Relaxing (hobbies, meditation, journaling, etc.)
❏ Making health-related appointments
❏ Figuring out living arrangements (apartment hunting, finding roommates, etc.)
❏ Other: _____

WORK/PROFESSIONAL
❏ Finding internships
❏ Making it to work on time
❏ Visiting the Career Services Center
❏ Preparing a resume
❏ Writing a cover letter

❏ Submitting application materials

❏ Preparing for interviews

❏ Finding a job

❏ Other:_____

FAMILY/SOCIAL/OTHER

❏ Talking with friends

❏ Keeping in touch with family members

❏ Responding to emails

❏ Going out/socializing

❏ Dating

❏ Ending a relationship

❏ Other: _____

❏ Other: _____

❏ Other: _____

Next, we dive into the procrastination flowchart. Identify the specific task you've been avoiding. To begin, ask yourself, "Am I actually working on this?" If yes, take a moment to reflect on your progress and clarify your goals. If no, consider what you're doing instead and the justifications you're using for your inaction. Move through the worksheet in order, being honest about your answers. This reflective process empowers you to develop effective strategies to overcome procrastination.

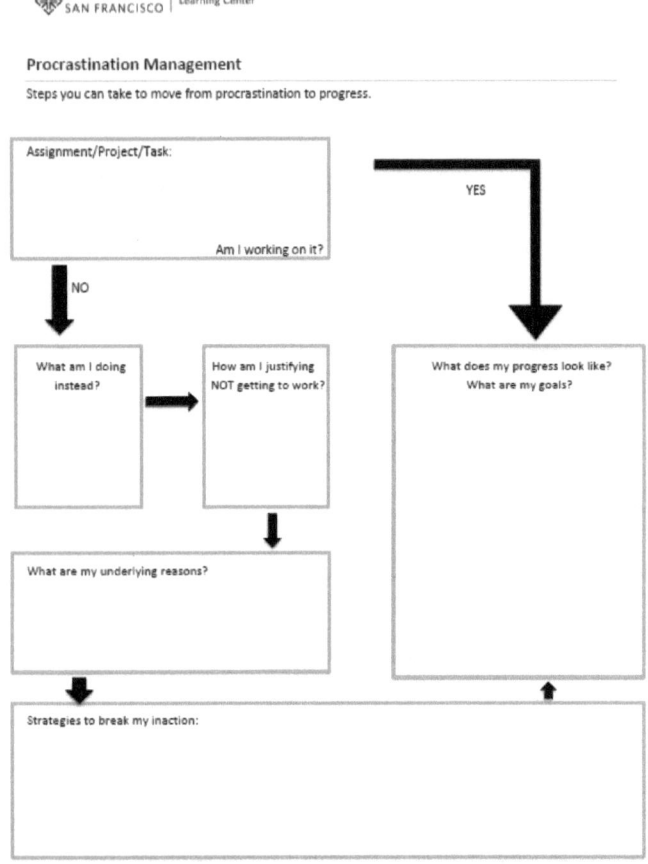

(Adapted from: The Academic Success Center, Oregon State University, 2010).

You'll see that one of the most important parts of the flowchart is the block that helps you identify strategies to break inaction. What works for one person may not work for another, but a common trick is to simply **break the task down into smaller, more manageable steps**. Then, set specific times for each step, and think about how to make these tasks more enjoyable. Establish small rewards for yourself upon completing each step to reinforce positive behavior.

Engaging in this comprehensive activity enables you to actively work on changing your procrastination patterns while cultivating a sense of joy and accomplishment throughout the process.

Looking Back, Looking Forward

Looking in a mirror often reflects only the surface, but the looking back/looking forward activity invites you to gaze deeper—into your past accomplishments and future aspirations. This exercise creates a meaningful connection between where you've been and where you want to go, offering a rare opportunity to pause, reflect, and set intentional goals. In a world that constantly urges us to focus on what's missing, this practice reminds us to appreciate our journey and envision a purposeful path ahead.

You may find value in combining this exercise with the life story exercise described in the previous section. This will provide a more visual aspect to the exercise.

If you prefer to simply use your journal, consider the following prompts:

Part 1: Looking Back

This part is about acknowledging your achievements and the lessons life has taught you. Too often we downplay our successes. Listing them out allows us to recognize our strengths and the resilience that has carried us through our past challenges. This reflection is not just about celebrating wins; it's a gratitude practice, honoring the wisdom gained from all experiences—big and small. Thinking of a particular period of time in your past:

- *List your accomplishments from this time, even if they seem minor.*
- *Describe an especially great day from this time.*
- *In what ways have you grown since then?*
- *What did you learn from that time?*
- *What challenges did you face and overcome back then? How?*

Part 2: Looking Forward

Here, you get to dream freely about the future. What goals light up your heart? What kind of person do you wish to become? Articulating these hopes and aspirations helps turn vague ideas into a clear roadmap, helping you align your journey with purpose and joy. Think about a specific point of time in the future:

- *What would you like to have achieved by that time, even if it's minor?*
- *What things are you looking forward to?*
- *What relationships would you like to begin or maintain?*
- *How will your life be different?*
- *What do you wish stays the same?*
- *What things are accessible and available to you that weren't before?*

You don't need to spend longer than ten minutes or so on this; plenty of insight can come from simply writing the first thing that pops into your mind. This activity is especially valuable during life's transitions—whether graduating, starting a family, or entering a new chapter. It empowers you to embrace your strengths and channel them into meaningful goals, solidifying your path through both reflection and future planning. Most importantly, it allows you to sidestep patterns of negativity, self-doubt, overthinking, and catastrophizing, all while encouraging a broader, more hopeful perspective.

Habit Tracking

Habits are the building blocks of personal growth, quietly shaping our lives one small action at a time. Unfortunately for many of us, anxiety and overthinking have become habits. We do it simply because we've always done it!

However, if it's possible to grow familiar with unhealthy habits, then we can do the same with healthy ones. It can be difficult at first to consistently remind yourself to do the things you know you should do, but **it's a question of awareness and staying mindful of your potential in any moment to make a better choice for yourself.**

A *habit tracker* is a simple yet powerful tool that helps you harness this potential, acting like a personal assistant that encourages you to improve every day. By monitoring your daily habits, a habit tracker keeps your goals visible and your progress measurable, whether you're aiming to jog each morning, read a chapter daily, meditate, or take your dog for a walk. It's a constant reminder of what truly matters to you.

Typically, a habit tracker takes the form of a chart or table, displaying the months and days alongside space for your specific habits. Each time you complete a habit, you mark it off on the chart, creating a visual record of your efforts.

Over time, this simple action becomes incredibly motivating, allowing you to see your progress take shape and fueling your commitment to keep going. You may start up a winning streak you're simply not willing to break!

But the benefits of a habit tracker go beyond just checking off boxes. Every time you mark a habit as complete, you experience a sense of accomplishment that boosts your confidence and reinforces positive behaviors. You are teaching your brain that doing healthy things *feels good*. It brings mindfulness to your daily routine, helping you notice patterns, adjust habits, and make choices that align with your goals. As you track habits regularly, you become more intentional about your actions, leading to healthier lifestyle changes over time.

In the end, a habit tracker transforms your journey toward self-improvement into an engaging, rewarding experience, helping you build consistency, sustain motivation, and deepen your connection to personal growth.

Developing A Growth Mindset

Our brains are wired to adapt, learn, and grow, but the key to unlocking this potential often lies in how we view challenges. This theory was first popularized by psychologist Carol Dweck; she claimed **a *growth mindset* is characterized by a core belief in the possibility of change and improvement.** A *fixed mindset*, on the other hand, is the core belief that one's traits are set in stone, and we cannot grow or develop beyond our innate abilities. The latter is most associated with depression, anxiety, lack of resilience and a host of negative psychological outcomes.

The growth mindset activity below (courtesy of growyourmindset.co.uk) is a powerful tool for nurturing the belief that your abilities can expand through hard work and persistence. Embracing a growth mindset transforms challenges into stepping stones for growth, encouraging you to see setbacks as temporary rather than permanent roadblocks. Instead of worrying and ruminating over things, we remember that we have the power to learn, to adapt, to improve ourselves, and to overcome– and this naturally lowers our anxiety levels.

It's all about confronting difficult situations rather than avoiding them, encouraging you to view challenges as temporary hurdles. The idea is to shift from fearing failure to embracing the learning that comes with it. By reflecting on these principles, you can reshape your thought patterns, adopting a more positive, proactive approach when things get tough.

For a week, pay attention to the fixed or growth mindset statements you hear—from yourself and those around you. This might include conversations with colleagues, family members, or even your own inner dialogue. By categorizing each statement as fixed (F), growth (G), or unsure (U), you'll begin to notice how language reflects and reinforces beliefs and attitudes.

Some examples:

Growth mindset

"Mistakes help me to learn."

"I haven't figured it out...yet."

"Who can I ask for help?"

"This may take some time."

"I'm learning, and that's OK."

"I'm on the right track."

Fixed mindset

"I just can't do it."

"I'm no good at XYZ."

"If I can't do it now, that means I won't ever do it."

"Why bother?"

"I'll never learn."

"This is just who I am."

"It's not supposed to be this hard."

"It's so embarrassing to fail."

This exercise goes beyond simple observation; it's an opportunity to engage in deeper reflection and conversation on how words shape our mindset. In recognizing these patterns, you empower yourself to foster a mindset rooted in growth, resilience, and the confidence that your potential is always evolving. Can you pick just one or two phrases that you can practice rephrasing in your everyday life? Instead of saying, "I suck at math" you could practice replacing it with, "I'm learning to be better at math." It makes a big difference!

Silver Linings

In difficult situations, **we have a choice: we can dwell on the negatives, or we can choose to look for the positives.** While it might not always feel like we have a choice in how we respond to adversity, with awareness and the willingness to change, we do. It's all a matter of deliberately choosing where to place your attention.

The silver linings: positive psychology exercise is designed to help you find those hidden gems of optimism even in challenging times. Research shows that identifying the silver linings of tough situations can lead to increased happiness and a more optimistic outlook on life. The more you practice this exercise, the easier it becomes to recognize the positives and foster a healthier mindset.

Start with a journal and a pen, and simply list five things that make your life enjoyable or worthwhile right now, big or small. These can range from simple pleasures, like enjoying a sunny day, to more significant things, such as supportive friendships or personal achievements. What's important is your mental orientation and perspective; this activity pushes you into a receptive, optimistic frame of mind where you're able to perceive all the good around you. This step sets a positive tone and reminds you of the good things in your life, creating a sense of gratitude. Basically, it's the perfect antidote to anxiety and doom-and-gloom style worry.

Next, describe a recent difficult situation or a time when things didn't go as planned. This reflection is essential, as it brings to light the challenges you face and allows you to process your feelings. Finally, spend time identifying and describing the silver linings of that past difficult situation. What lessons did you learn? How did you eventually overcome it? Were there unexpected benefits or moments of growth that emerged from the struggle?

Regularly practicing this exercise helps you develop the habit of finding silver linings, which is associated with decreased depression, improved coping abilities, and increased relationship satisfaction. It may not feel especially natural at first, but with time it will become much easier to consider the upside in everything you do. By embracing this mindset, you'll cultivate resilience and a deeper sense of gratitude for life's journey.

Personal Strengths Inventory

Sometimes, stress and anxiety come down to a faulty appraisal we've made of life: we have estimated that the threats and dangers out there are very serious indeed, *and* that we ourselves are weak, vulnerable, or unable to cope with those challenges. But is it really true that we are powerless in the face of adversity? Is it really true that we are not up to the challenges of life?

The personal strengths inventory is here to help you explore and celebrate the qualities that set you apart. What makes you unique? What do you bring to the world that nobody else can? In a world that often highlights flaws, this exercise encourages you to focus on your strengths, giving you the opportunity to recognize and honor all the positive traits you bring to the table.

As you move through the inventory below, you'll find a list of personal qualities that may resonate with you. Feel free to choose as many as you feel apply and add any that you feel are missing. This exercise goes beyond simply ticking boxes—it's about reflecting deeply on the strengths that define you. By circling or highlighting attributes that truly matter in your life, you create a powerful reminder of your worth and potential.

Wisdom	Self-control	Leadership	Patience
Curiosity	Assertiveness	Love	Persistence
Creativity	Flexibility	Forgiveness	Intelligence
Empathy	Humor	Confidence	Cooperation
Resilience	Common sense	Modesty	Open-mindedness
Bravery	Discernment	Honesty	Adventurousness
Discipline	Logic	Spirituality	Social awareness

This reflection extends to different areas of your life, inviting you to see how your strengths impact your relationships, work, and personal fulfillment.

For relationships, ask yourself:

What qualities help me connect meaningfully with others?

How can I use these strengths to enhance my bonds with friends and family?

In your career, consider:

How do my strengths contribute to my work?

How have they helped me overcome challenges or achieve goals?

When it comes to personal growth, think about:

Which strengths bring me joy?

How can I pursue my passions with more focus and confidence?

Life's demands can often feel overwhelming, but this inventory serves as a powerful reminder of your inherent abilities. Embracing your strengths not only boosts your confidence but also prepares you to tackle challenges head-on. So take a moment to dive into this exercise, allowing it to guide you toward a more fulfilling and empowered life.

Replacing What If Statements

What-ifs are thoughts that can spiral into a maze of catastrophic thinking, often amplifying anxiety and fear. The replacing what-if statements activity is a valuable process designed to help you navigate this mental maze and reduce stress.

To start, you need to identify and express your what-if fears. For example, you might worry about not performing well in a job interview. Recognizing these specific anxieties is the crucial first step in addressing them directly. Face them and own up to them honestly and without judgment.

Next, try to transform those nagging what-if questions into clear, factual statements about your experiences. Instead of remaining trapped in the loop of "What if I don't get the job?" you might shift your focus to, "I didn't get the job." This change grounds your thoughts in reality, helping to lighten the emotional burden those fears carry.

In the face of the unknown, we need to routinely pull ourselves back to what we *do* know–and let go of the rest. Instead of saying, "What if it's cancer?" just focus on what is absolutely true and known about the here and now. "There is absolutely no evidence that I have cancer. I feel fine right now." Instead of saying, "What if they're all secretly laughing at me?" you could ground back in reality by saying only what you know for sure: "When I left the party yesterday they all said they had a good time and they told me to come again. That's all that actually happened."

The third step encourages you to challenge these statements with reflective questions. Think about your past experiences: Have you faced similar situations before? What was the outcome? Were things as bad as you predicted? Was there an upside you didn't notice at first? Did the worst thing happen after all?

This critical thinking helps you gain perspective on your fears, allowing you to see them more clearly. Consider asking yourself what evidence supports or contradicts these fears; this insight can be truly enlightening.

Finally, you'll reframe those what-if statements into balanced, positive thoughts. Rather than fixating on worst-case scenarios, tell yourself, "I am well-prepared for the interview," or "I have the skills they're looking for." An optional next step is to turn what-if statements completely on their head and ask yourself, "What if something really wonderful happens? What if this all goes really well?"

This activity not only cultivates a healthier mindset, but it also empowers you to tackle challenges with confidence and optimism. By practicing this exercise regularly, you can reshape your thought patterns, approaching life's uncertainties with calm and resilience. The next time you hear yourself thinking, "What if...," quickly pause, connect to *what is*, and then challenge yourself to imagine that, just possibly, a good thing may happen, too.

Focusing On Little Things

Humans sometimes focus on the big things, overlooking the small joys that fill our everyday lives. The focus on the little things activity invites you to embrace mindfulness and find happiness in these ordinary moments, echoing the philosophy of ikigai—the belief that our lives can be enriched with purpose and joy. At its core, ikigai teaches us that true fulfillment often lies in the simplest tasks, whether it's savoring a cup of tea or diving into a work project.

To get started, take a moment the night before to jot down four activities you typically do on autopilot the next day. These could be as simple as making breakfast, brushing your teeth, or going for a walk. As you consider each activity, immerse yourself in the details. For instance, when preparing a cup of tea, notice how the cup feels in your hands, inhale the rich aroma, and appreciate the warmth of the water. Observing how your hands move and watching the water swirl can transform a routine task into a mindful experience.

It's not important that any of these activities are super entertaining or mind-blowing–the value comes in your heightened awareness and appreciation, and your ability to slow down and fully engage with the moment. You may discover that your anxious thoughts are much less pronounced if you can spend even a few minutes in this state of mind a couple of times a day.

It may be beneficial to end the exercise by journalling and writing down what you experienced during each activity, noting the smells, sounds, textures, and tastes. This practice encourages you to stay aware and connect fully with the present moment. By focusing on the little things, you'll discover that even the simplest actions can bring profound joy and fulfillment to your life. All this can be done when you **get out of your head and into the moment**!

The magic of this exercise also lies in the accumulation of small joys, much like we experimented with using the gratitude jar. Finding happiness in simple actions—like starting his day with a cup of coffee and chocolate—can significantly enhance your daily experience. By turning these moments into pleasurable encounters, you set a positive tone for your day and cultivate a deeper appreciation for the beauty in everyday life. Breathe out, relax, and **just be** for a moment. Isn't it interesting how you can experience feelings of total immersion and infinite expansiveness, in something as simple as washing your coffee mug at 10am on a Tuesday?

Section 4: Self-Care Practices for Healing and Repair

Self-Care Check-in

Remember the analogy we used earlier in this book, where anxiety was likened to a flashing light on the dashboard of a car? The following exercise is a little like tuning in with yourself to see exactly why the check engine light is on, whether the tank is full, and whether the back seat needs a quick vacuum!

When life gets too busy, we often forget to check in with ourselves and prioritize our own well-being. We might not even notice that we are getting steadily more tired, depleted, or overwhelmed. Too many of us wait until we're badly out of balance to take action, and by then, it's often too late.

The self-care check-in activity is a fantastic way to dive into what self-care truly means to you, and to help you learn to course-correct in small, everyday ways. This exercise serves as a reminder that self-care is deeply personal; what nourishes one person may not resonate with another, and that's OK.

Start by evaluating specific self-care areas of your life, such as:

- Spending quality time with family
- Carving out moments for yourself

- Engaging in activities that bring you joy
- Taking care of your environment and your health
- Maintaining or creating new friendships
- Keeping up with life maintenance, hygiene, and practical routines

Carefully consider how well you are taking care of yourself in each area. By rating each area in turn, you can easily identify where you're thriving and where you might need to give yourself a little extra love.

Next, explore ways to give yourself a little bit more of the support you need. Remember, this will really depend on you as an individual. Consider going for a walk, meditating, or listening to your favorite music. You could declutter your closet or cozy up with a good show. Don't underestimate the joy of doing yoga, enjoying a snack, or sipping a refreshing drink of water. You might even start a new hobby or connect with a friend over coffee, creating moments that recharge your spirit.

After completing your check-in, take a moment to reflect. What patterns do you notice in your responses? Is there anything you can do to prioritize self-care more? How can you prevent burnout moving forward? Regularly engaging in this activity helps you cultivate a proactive approach to mental wellness, reminding you that even the smallest actions can lead to a happier, more balanced life.

My Self-Care Promise

Committing to take care of yourself is one of the most important vows you can make, especially when life gets tough. Instead of worrying and heaping on self-blame and negative self-talk, why not make the pledge to be kind to yourself, and to give yourself the things you need?

The self-care promise exercise is a powerful way to connect with yourself, regardless of who you are or what your limitations are. Think of it as a personal commitment to prioritize your well-being, particularly during those challenging moments when anxiety or depression might threaten to pull you down. It's all too easy to let self-care slip through the cracks when life feels overwhelming, but this practice encourages you to reflect on what truly nurtures your spirit.

Start by considering the times when your self-care might falter. Be honest–when are the times in life you're most likely to put yourself and your wellbeing at the bottom of the list? What might trigger you to self-neglect?

Once you've identified these scenarios, you can be prepared by choosing a mantra ahead of time. **This mantra is a gentle reminder to treat yourself with the kindness and compassion you deserve-no matter what.** Format it in an "if–then" structure; it's akin to crafting a game plan for when life throws you curveballs. For example, "If I feel ill or unwell, then I will take the time needed to get better again, without guilt."

You can also begin by affirming your commitment with statements like, "I promise myself that...," This declaration sets a powerful intention, guiding you to think about what you genuinely need. Reflect on questions like: "When I'm feeling sad, I will remember...," and "The next time I feel anxious, I will...." These reflections empower you to acknowledge your feelings and respond with grace and understanding.

Consider how you'll manage stress: "When I feel lost or stressed, I will stop and remind myself...," and "If I find myself making excuses, I will...." This process isn't just about accountability; it's about creating a proactive approach to self-care that puts you back in control. The next time the check engine light flashes, you'll know exactly how to respond.

Nurturing vs. Depleting Activities

Those of us who are professional worriers may be in the habit of everyday martyrdom–we persist in tasks, thoughts, and activities that make us feel bad, drain us, and wear us down. **Our anxiety is like a dripping tap that slowly drains away our energy. What if, instead, we**

found ways to fill ourselves up, one drop at a time?

Understanding the difference between nurturing and depleting activities is essential when taking care of ourselves. *Nurturing activities* are the ones that lift our spirits and energize us—think about the joy of diving into a favorite hobby, spending quality time with friends, or savoring a comforting cup of tea. These little moments add up, contributing to our happiness and helping us manage stress effectively.

On the flip side, *depleting activities* can really drain us. These might include repetitive tasks at work, endless caregiving responsibilities, or getting caught up in negative news cycles. When life feels overwhelming, it's all too easy to focus solely on what we have to do, often sidelining the activities that truly nourish our souls.

Finding the right balance between these two types of activities is essential. By making room for more nurturing moments, we can boost our overall well-being and resilience.

That's where the nurturing vs. depleting activities exercise comes in. It's simple: draw a line down the middle of a blank page to create two columns. On one side, list activities that deplete you, and on the other, activities that nurture and energize you. You may be surprised to find that some activities can fall on both sides of the page!

This simple exercise will give you a clearer picture of how you spend your time, and will help you identify where you can sprinkle in more uplifting activities. Can you do a little more of one and a little less of the other? Ultimately, it empowers you to create a healthier balance in your life, making every day a little brighter.

Healthy Meal Planning

How much of your daily anxiety and stress comes from *food*? Whether that's eating, cooking, shopping, or cleaning up after meals, food plays a big role in our lives. Depending on your approach, it can be a depleting or a nurturing activity.

You are what you eat, and the choices you make in the kitchen can significantly impact your overall well-being. The meal planning and preparation activity is a game-changer that can transform not just your diet, but also your mindset. Research shows that dedicating time to plan your meals can reduce stress and boost your self-esteem. Why? Because having control over your food choices turns mealtime into a more positive experience, making it easier to steer clear of disordered eating habits.

One of the greatest advantages of meal planning is the time and energy it saves. Imagine not having to scramble at the last minute to figure out what to eat. Instead, you can relax, knowing your meals are already prepped and ready to go. This thoughtful approach eliminates decision fatigue, allowing you to enjoy a more relaxed dining experience. Food becomes a source of joy and fulfilment again.

Let's not overlook the financial benefits! Planning your meals and buying ingredients in bulk can save you a significant amount on groceries and dining out. This not only lessens your expenditures, but it also contributes to a sense of financial stability—who doesn't want that?

Moreover, when you plan your meals ahead of time, you're more likely to make healthier choices. With everything laid out, you can select nourishing ingredients that fuel your body and mind. This leads to improved physical health, greater mental clarity, and increased energy, helping you feel your best.

There is no right way to meal plan; everyone is different. However, you can make a start by simply taking steps to **plan ahead for just the next three meals**. A little bit of effort spent learning how to shop, put meals together, and stock your pantry intelligently will pay huge dividends, and cut your stress in half. It doesn't need to be fancy–you could even batch cook and have the same meal a few nights in a row.

Meal planning isn't just about food; it's about creating a healthier, happier life. By investing a little time in preparation, you set the stage for success every day, ensuring that your meals support not just your hunger, but your overall well-being.

Two-Week Sleep Diary

Have you ever thought: "I wish I could just turn my brain off sometimes"?

Well, you can–and you should. During sleep!

Sleep is essential to our well-being, yet many of us struggle to get the restful nights we need. It can become a vicious cycle: poor sleep reinforces bad sleep habits, which cause poor sleep, and so on. If you spend the night doomscrolling on your phone, for example, you feed your anxiety and set yourself up for a terrible night's sleep. In the morning, your sleep deficit means you're more likely to focus on the negative, to resort to unhealthy coping mechanisms, and to feel overwhelmed. In other words–you're more prone to anxiety, and more sensitive to its effects. Then, because you spend the entire day stressed out in this way, you reach the evening feeling burnt out and wanting to just "relax" a little… and the easiest thing in the world is to pull out your phone and start doomscrolling again…

The two-week sleep diary is like your personal sleep detective, helping you unravel the mystery of your nightly rest. By dedicating 14 days to track your sleep habits, you can uncover those sneaky patterns that disrupt your slumber, and discover ways to reclaim your nights.

Each day, you'll become a mindful observer of your bedtime rituals. Write down the essentials: how long you actually slept, and what time you decided to call it a night. Pay attention to any nighttime interruptions—how many times did you wake up, and how long did it take to drift back off? It's also crucial to note the caffeine and alcohol you consumed, any medications you took, and whether you carved out time for exercise.

Think of this as a sleep diary adventure. You might stumble upon revelations like that afternoon espresso sabotaging your sleep or those late-night scrolling sessions keeping you wide awake. Identifying these little culprits empowers you to make conscious changes and reclaim the restful nights you deserve.

Each week, take a moment to reflect on your findings. What habits stood out to you? How can you tweak your routine for better sleep? This isn't just about logging your nights; it's about embracing the journey toward healthier sleep habits. With a little dedication and introspection, you're not just tracking sleep—you're crafting a path toward vibrant days and peaceful nights, setting the stage for a life filled with energy and clarity. So, grab that diary and get ready to transform your relationship with sleep!

Movement Breaks

Not moving can take a toll on your health and well-being, especially when you're glued to a desk for hours on end. In the moment, you may start to feel sluggish and depleted, and your thoughts may tend towards complaining and griping, but **many of these cognitive and emotional effects really begin as physiological effects.** Because we are physically tired and immobile, our thoughts and feelings are similarly stagnant.

The movement breaks activity is your invitation to step away from that desk and shake off the cobwebs. Research shows that prolonged sitting isn't just uncomfortable; it's a significant health risk. It's linked to obesity, heart disease, diabetes, and even some types of cancer. By incorporating movement into your day, you not only boost your health but also enhance your productivity at work. And for those of us constantly on the go, taking a moment to stretch, relax, or reflect can create valuable headspace for tackling the next task.

So, why should you prioritize movement breaks? First off, they help reduce blood pooling and causing swelling in your legs and feet. They also promote increased physical activity in general and encourage you to get more steps in throughout the day. Plus, a little movement can significantly improve your focus and overall mental clarity while you work, leading to a healthier work-life balance.

But what exactly is a *movement break*? It's a mindful pause of about 5–10 minutes where you step away from your sedentary routine. This could mean taking a brisk walk, doing some light exercises, or even breaking a sweat with some higher-intensity movements. The goal is to get your blood flowing, lower the risks associated with inactivity, and boost your energy levels.

To get started, read through the different types of exercises available in the worksheet. Choose 1–3 from each category, aiming for 2-3 sets of 10 repetitions. Begin with just one movement break a day and gradually carve out more time for movement throughout your day. Your body—and mind—will thank you!

Digital Detox

We can't talk about self-care without giving proper consideration to one of the most ubiquitous parts of modern life: screens and technology. Screens have become an integral part of our lives, but sometimes, they can overwhelm us. It's simply no longer an option to be passive about media consumption and the impacts technology has on life.

A *digital detox* **is an intentional break from screens and digital devices, allowing you to reassess your relationship with technology.** In our fast-paced world, where smartphones and computers often dominate our attention, stepping away can be refreshing. It's a chance to unplug from the constant buzz of notifications and social media, helping you reconnect with the real world and yourself.

During a digital detox, you can choose to limit your use of technology. This might involve designating specific tech-free hours, avoiding social media altogether, or creating spaces in your home where devices are not allowed. All that matters is that there are *limits*, and that these limits have been consciously and deliberately initiated by you, for your own benefit. By doing this, you create room for clarity and reflection, allowing yourself to focus on activities that genuinely bring you joy. You put yourself back in control, so that you are using your time, attention, energy, and resources in a way that reflects your values and honors your goals. Whether it's picking up a book, enjoying nature, or spending quality time with loved ones, a break from screens can help you engage more fully with life around you.

The way that you choose to do a detox will depend on your unique lifestyle, but here are some ideas to practice implementing today:

- Explore old screen-free hobbies you may have forgotten about
- Pick a "lights-out" time every evening, and ban screens beyond that point
- Take up old fashioned letter writing or phone calls to stay in touch with people
- Commit to checking your inbox just once or twice at a fixed time per day
- Stay accountable to a friend and see if you can detox together for support

Seek help from a therapist if addiction is at play

It's a good idea to keep a digital detox diary, whether you're detoxing for a day or a month or more. By tracking your progress and reflecting on how these changes impact your mood and productivity, you can better understand the benefits of stepping back from technology.

Ultimately, a digital detox is about finding balance. It allows you to reclaim your time and energy, fostering a healthier relationship with technology while enhancing your overall well-being. Taking this time for yourself can lead to a more fulfilling and connected life.

Positive Self-Talk Exercise

It's one thing to cut down on the digital noise and distraction from out there in the world, but what about all the noise and chatter *inside* your head?

Imagine you're sitting quietly, and all you can hear is that nagging voice in your head, criticizing every little thing about you. You could be in a beautiful, tranquil spot with a loved one–but if your mind is anxious, it doesn't matter.

Now, what if you could flip that script? Self-talk is not the problem. Rather, it's the content of what we tell ourselves, day in and day out. What if, instead of self-doubt, your inner dialogue was a source of encouragement and strength? That's the magic of positive self-talk, an activity that's all about nurturing kindness and compassion towards yourself.

We're often great at being kind to others, but how often do we treat ourselves with the same level of care? The way we talk to ourselves can significantly impact our mood and self-worth. For instance, when you're faced with a tough challenge, it's easy to spiral into thoughts like, "I can't do this." Negative self-talk can chip away at our confidence and ramp up our anxiety, leaving us feeling defeated.

This activity encourages you to pay attention to your self-talk. Take (non-judgmental) note of your thoughts throughout the day–whether mentally or in a journal. Are they more positive or negative? Analyze these thoughts—are they even true? Dig into the emotions behind them; they can reveal what you truly need.

Then, it's time to reframe those negative thoughts into something kinder. Swap "I'm not good enough" for "I'm learning and improving." Finally, sprinkle positive affirmations into your daily routine. This isn't just a mental exercise; it's a powerful form of self-care. This can feel challenging, but even a little push-back against habitual negative self-talk can begin to help loosen its influence on you.

Be nice to yourself! By nurturing yourself with compassion, you can build your self-esteem and reduce anxiety. Remember, you deserve to be as kind to yourself as you are to your friends!

Write a Letter to Your Past and Future Self

Can you remember what you were like as a teenager?

Can you recall all the things that bothered you back then? Chances are, you have quite a different perspective on all those things now! This exercise is about trying to find a little of that same perspective on your life's problems, only right now, in the present.

Writing letters to your future and past selves opens up a beautiful avenue for introspection, allowing you to explore who you are, who you've been, and who you want to become. Recall that anxiety is about narrowing attention; it creates tunnel vision that makes us believe that nothing else exists except the thing we are worried about right now.

When you write to your future self, it's like crafting a personal vision board with words. It invites you to take a broader, more expanded view, and gives you perspective. Picture this: you're dreaming about the life you want to create in five years. What accomplishments do you hope to celebrate? What kind of relationships do you want to nurture? This exercise isn't just about wishful thinking; it's about setting intentions and mapping out the steps you need to take today to make those dreams a reality.

Writing to your past self can feel like giving your younger self a warm hug. It's a chance to reflect on the challenges and victories that have shaped your journey. You can share insights, remind yourself of the resilience you've shown, and offer kindness to the person you once were. This reflection helps you understand how your past influences your present, and helps guide your future choices.

These letter-writing exercises are like a personal time capsule for your thoughts and feelings. By reaching out to your past and future selves, you get a chance to reflect on your journey and dream about where you want to go. It's a way to check in with yourself, to understand how far you've come and to remind yourself of the person you want to be. One particularly fascinating possibility is going back to read your letters in a week, a month or a year. You may be surprised at the effect that time has had on your outlook!

Self-Esteem Stems

We often underestimate the power of our inner dialogue. Perhaps we have become so accustomed to our inner voice and all the things it says, that we forget that it's a voice at all, and we merely assume it's just reality itself that we are perceiving.

Have you ever considered how your self-talk has shaped and influenced your reality?

The self-esteem sentence stems exercise is designed to guide you through a simple yet impactful sentence completion activity. It invites you to engage with prompts, allowing you to express your thoughts and feelings in a way that feels authentic to you. This isn't just about filling in the blanks; it's an opportunity to dive deep into your inner dialogue.

Completing this exercise can be incredibly freeing. It encourages you to explore your emotions and thoughts, making it easier to share them with others. As you work through the prompts, you may find yourself becoming more comfortable discussing your feelings, which is a crucial step in addressing self-esteem challenges. It's all about building that bridge to self-acceptance. The prompts below are a great start:

I have always wished I could...

I'm secretly terrified of...

Today I would enjoy doing...

I look forward to...

I feel something that the future holds for me is...

I get my courage/purpose/inspiration from...

Something I couldn't live without is...

I would never...

It made me feel happy when...

I love it when...

I find it difficult to...

It makes me so angry when...

Something I truly desire is...

I thrive in life when...

This week I hope to...

Something I secretly think is...

I find it tricky to admit...

To get the most out of this activity, set aside 5-10 minutes several times a week for reflection and completion. Do all the prompts, or focus on just one or two that resonate deeply. After two weeks of consistent practice, take a moment to review what you've written. This reflection allows you to gain valuable insights into your outlook on life and helps you recognize how your mindset has evolved since you began.

The aim here is to watch your answers gradually shift toward a more positive perspective, fostering a healthier self-image over time. By completing these sentences, you can cultivate a deeper understanding of yourself and take meaningful steps toward enhancing your self-esteem.

Bibliotherapy

If you're reading this book right now, you probably are already a believer in the power of bibliotherapy! **Books have the incredible power to heal and transform our lives.** *Bibliotherapy* harnesses this magic by using literature as a therapeutic tool to help navigate emotions like anxiety, depression, and grief. The right kind of reading allows you to connect with stories that resonate with your experiences, guiding you toward greater self-awareness and understanding.

To start your bibliotherapy journey, reflect on the challenges you're currently facing. Write down the central issues in your life, then pick one that you'd most like to address. Next, explore a curated list of books tailored to your needs—whether it's *Everything I Never Told You* by Celeste Ng for depression, *Turtles All the Way Down* by John Green for anxiety, or *A Monster Calls* by Patrick Ness for grief.

Take your time when picking a book. What matters is that it's the right book for you as a person, in the place where you are right now. Consult lists online, ask friends for recommendations, or use the power of algorithms to help you identify materials similar to what you've enjoyed before. Check reviews and summaries, and if possible, read a small sample first to see whether the book suits your needs.

Once you've selected a book, set aside dedicated time to read it thoughtfully. As you delve into the story, take notes on any strategies, insights, or approaches that resonate with you. Pause often to reflect. These reflections can be invaluable in helping you tackle the issues you're contending with. **Imagine that you are actually conversing with your book**–ask questions, argue, paraphrase. When you're done with the book, choose one key strategy, approach, or insight that speaks to you and create a realistic plan to incorporate it into your daily life.

Keep a journal to monitor your progress, making simple notes about your journey along the way.

At the end of each week, review your notes and adjust your plan if necessary. Throughout this process, remember to be gentle with yourself—facing your emotions takes courage, and each step forward is a testament to your inner strength and resilience.

Learning Self-Forgiveness

Forgiving yourself can be hard, especially when the weight of past mistakes lingers. It may sound obvious, but we can never change the past, no matter how well we do right now, in the present. **Forgiveness, then, is an unavoidable necessity**–especially if we wish to continue developing throughout life.

Learning self-forgiveness is an empowering exercise that encourages you to confront and release the burden of regret. While everyone makes errors, the real challenge lies in moving forward rather than getting stuck in guilt and shame. To err is human, but it takes a deliberate effort to properly process those mistakes and move on from them as best as we can. This exercise emphasizes accepting responsibility for your actions while practicing kindness toward yourself, ultimately leading to emotional healing. The process begins with the 4 R's of self-forgiveness: accept responsibility, express remorse, repair the damage and restore trust, and renewal.

First, **Accept Responsibility**. Acknowledge your role in what happened. This can often be the hardest step. It's time to stop making excuses and face the reality of your choices with honesty. This alone can be incredibly freeing!

Next, **Express Remorse**. It's natural to feel guilt and shame, so allow yourself to experience these emotions. Forcing "toxic positivity" may be counterproductive here–try to avoid rushing this step, as unpleasant as it may be. Journaling or writing a letter can help articulate your feelings and enhance self-awareness during this reflective process.

The third step is to **Repair the Damage and Restore Trust**. Making amends is essential for self-forgiveness. Apologizing to those you've hurt or finding ways to make it right can help you release guilt and begin the healing process more effectively. You may not be able to do much practically, in which case self-forgiveness or participating in a reconciliatory action may be helpful.

Finally, focus on **Renewal**. Instead of dwelling on negativity, reflect on what you can learn from the experience. Transform the mistake into something valuable. Understanding your choices can prevent similar situations in the future and promote personal growth.

The above four steps can be explored in a journal and can help shape your behavior in a situation or relationship. What's important is that all four of these elements are present to permit healing. By the end, you'll gain insights into your emotions and learn how to move forward with self-compassion and clarity, ultimately nurturing your emotional well-being.

Lose the Mask!

In the last section, we briefly mentioned the importance of avoiding toxic positivity, which is really nothing more than inauthenticity, and an unwillingness to face and accept the present reality for what it really is.

Sometimes, we like to pretend as if we're wearing masks to conceal our true selves. This can also extend to pretending to be more emotionally together than we are, braver, kinder, or somehow less vulnerable or unsure than we really are.

Emotion masks serve a similar purpose, allowing us to hide our genuine feelings beneath an invisible facade. Just like the masks we don when acting or dressing up, these emotional shields can protect us from vulnerability, but they can also prevent us from being authentic.

We often wear emotion masks without even realizing it. When we keep our feelings hidden or act in ways that don't align with our true emotions, we're essentially donning a mask. For example, you might pretend to be happy when you're actually feeling down, or you might say you're fine when inside, you're worried. Maybe you act indifferent about something bothering you, or you express anger even when sadness is what you're really feeling.

The lose the mask activity encourages you to think about how you manage your feelings in front of others. It highlights that we all "wear masks" at times to hide our true emotions. For instance, you might act fine when you're not, or show anger when you actually feel hurt.

To get started, take a moment to reflect on the kinds of emotion masks you wear. **What do you hide behind?**

Since it can be difficult to put into words, try sketching and drawing your mask first, on a simple sheet of paper. Draw the expression and use colors and other symbols, if you like. This allows you to visualize what you're revealing, but also what you're concealing. As you draw, ask what lies underneath the mask. What is hidden? What is being protected? What would you like to show people more of?

By putting your creativity and imagination to use, you can explore all the moments you've put on a mask to hide how you truly feel.

Self-Love Journal

Many of us cringe at the concept of "self-love." Isn't that just vanity or narcissism? The answer is *no*!

Learning to genuinely love yourself can be one of the most transformative journeys you take. **A self-love journal helps you cultivate more self-compassion, and encourages more genuine emotional expression. It's a way to keep track of your developing relationship with yourself.** Carve out a few moments each day to reflect on your unique qualities and achievements, helping you highlight the wonderful traits that often get overlooked in the chaos of daily life.

Self-love journaling is a powerful way to remind yourself of your strengths and the positives surrounding you. This acts as a counterbalance to any negative self-talk, and reminds you to go easy on yourself. Take a few prompts each day, or focus on just one that stands out to you.

Here are some to get you started:

- What is one thing you really like about yourself? Why?

- What are some personal traits that you're grateful to have?
- What is something you can forgive yourself for today?
- What was a compliment you received in the past? How did it make you feel?
- What were some challenges in the past that you successfully overcame? How did you overcome them?
- What do you bring to the world that no other person can?
- What are you proud of yourself for doing?
- What is one way you can be nice to yourself today? What makes you feel really good? Can you find a way to do some of that soon?

Journaling can be an intimate space for self-reflection, allowing you to explore where you can sprinkle more kindness and compassion into your life. It's also a fantastic outlet for emotional expression, serving as a mood booster or a way to unwind after a long day. For example, recalling joyful moments can help you pinpoint what you want more of, while reflecting on your accomplishments can really lift your spirits.

To get started, find a quiet moment that feels right, whether it's during your morning coffee or as you wind down for the night. Use the prompts as a springboard for your thoughts, or come up with your own! Aim to write something every day. This simple yet meaningful practice can greatly enhance your sense of self-worth and happiness, reminding you of the love you truly deserve.

Catch Yourself Being Great

We don't notice it, but sometimes we suck at giving ourselves the credit we deserve! Especially if anxiety is a personal challenge for us, we can tend to focus on the negative while completely ignoring all the blessings, good fortune, advantages, and opportunities all around us.

Catch yourself being great is a fun and engaging way to boost your positive self-regard through the power of positive reinforcement. This exercise invites you to celebrate your achievements and good deeds in a creative way, helping you cultivate a mindset of appreciation for yourself. Plus, it's fun!

The first step is to create your own reward jar. Grab some pens, stickers, or any art supplies you have on hand, and transform a simple jar into a beautiful container for storing important messages. This jar will become a visual reminder of your accomplishments and the positive actions you take.

Next, create a "Monthly Good Deeds" calendar and fill it in for the corresponding month. This is exactly the same as a normal calendar, only it's dedicated purely to the task of tracking all the good things you do every day for yourself and others.

It's simple: each time you do something good for yourself or someone else, add a gold star to that day on the calendar. If you're unsure of what qualifies as a good deed, don't worry; examples are provided to inspire you. Good deeds don't have to be big to make a difference–small things count, too. Maybe you went to the gym, helped a family member, did a self-love exercise, or pushed through your procrastination to complete a task.

As you add each star, place a specified amount of money into your reward jar. By the end of the month, you can use that money to treat yourself to something special. What that is depends on you! This exercise is grounded in classic behavioral research by B. F. Skinner, who showed that rewarding positive behaviors increases the likelihood of those behaviors being repeated.

The benefits of positive reinforcement extend beyond just personal growth; studies have found that it can encourage prosocial behaviors in both children and adults. The goal is to gradually shift your awareness onto the positive and reinforce the behaviors you know you want to cement in your own life.

Section 5: Inspirational Mindsets, Affirmations, and Models

Quote Reflection

There's a reason why quotes are so popular with so many people–they quickly and succinctly capture powerful messages of hope, inspiration, purpose, and more. Have you ever read a quote that resonated with you so deeply that it felt like it was speaking directly to your soul? Why not use that power more deliberately?

Reflecting on a quote offers a meaningful opportunity to explore your thoughts and uncover ideas that can reshape your understanding of the world. This isn't just about memorizing words or tired cliches; it's about connecting with the message on a personal level and digging into your own beliefs and experiences. **Quotes can become mantras and focal points for your deeper intentions.**

Your mind is a powerful tool, always seeking purpose and clarity. When you take the time to reflect on a quote, it acts like a net, catching those fleeting thoughts and feelings. Writing them down helps you transform these ideas into something tangible and new. It's a chance to articulate your insights, and in doing so, you contribute to the rich tapestry of human experience.

Taking ownership of your thoughts is a vital step toward embracing your individuality. Our reflections shape who we are, and through this process, we can transform past pains into hope, enriching our lives with purpose and meaning.

For this activity, choose a favorite quote or go hunting for a new one that speaks to you. Take the time to dive into what the quote you choose means to you on a deeper level. Consider the following reflective questions:

- *What does this quote mean to you?*
- *What was a time when you experienced this type of moment with another person?*
- *What feelings, thoughts, images, ideas, and concepts does this quote trigger for you?*
- *How did it make you feel to know that someone else was having a similar experience as you?*

Don't be afraid to dig deep—trust that something valuable will emerge. If you hit a wall, step away for a bit, do something else, and come back with fresh eyes. What you might like to do is print out your quote and hang it somewhere prominent, or write it at the top of a journal page.

Dear Me

In a previous section, you took the time to write letters to your past and future selves, diving into lessons learned and dreams yet to come. Now, let's shift the spotlight to your present self with the dear me activity. This reflective exercise invites you to connect with who you are right now, offering a valuable opportunity to acknowledge your current feelings, challenges, and victories.

Life can be busy, confusing and stressful. Even with the best of intentions, it can sometimes feel like we are rushing through life, never really taking the time to pause, reflect, and *process* what is going on for us. Taking the time to write to yourself is a way of giving yourself the space and opportunity to do so.

Writing a letter to yourself can be incredibly powerful, and its a great stress-relief technique. It's a chance to express your thoughts and emotions in a way that encourages self-compassion and understanding. Think about what you need to hear at this moment. Are you feeling overwhelmed, excited, or maybe a little lost? This letter is your safe space to spill it all out—no judgment, just honesty.

As you write, reflect on what you want to celebrate about yourself today. What are you proud of? What struggles are you facing, and how can you recognize your own resilience? This exercise helps you validate your experiences, giving you the chance to appreciate your growth and aspirations. There are no super-strict rules and formulas–simply speak your heart and be honest. **Start with "dear me,"**

and go from there. What do you most want to communicate to yourself, now that you're listening?

The dear me activity isn't just about writing; it's about connecting deeply with your present self and nurturing a sense of self-awareness and acceptance. Allow yourself the freedom to be vulnerable in this moment. Remember, this letter is for your eyes only, a reflection of your true self at this point in your journey. Embrace the opportunity to explore your thoughts and feelings, as this process can foster greater understanding and compassion for who you are today.

The Happy News Challenge

Do you have an anxiety problem... or have you just spent too long online?

Are you struggling with overthinking... or have you just been reading too much doom-and-gloom in the news?

When you turn on the TV or scroll through social media, it's often filled with bad news that can weigh heavily on your mental headspace. Even psychologically resilient and happy people can struggle if they consume too much of this relentlessly negative content.

That's why the happy news challenge activity is such a refreshing change! This fun exercise encourages you to focus on the positive by reporting a happy news story that brings a smile to your face—something uplifting or humorous to share with family and friends. Talk about countercultural!

To get started, think about where you might find a happy news story. You could explore sites like Newsround or First News, or even look for uplifting tales in your own community. Have you witnessed any good deeds or funny moments recently? Those little gems can make great stories!

Once you've chosen a story, gather the essential details using the 5 Ws: Who is involved? What happened? Where did it take place? When did it occur? Why is it significant? Has somebody done something praiseworthy and encouraging, or has there been a little flicker of humanity and good humor somewhere? Document it! To make your report even more engaging, find an interesting quote from someone connected to the story.

Now it's time to share your story! You can write it out as if for a family newsletter, video record it to share with your loved ones, or even audio record it for a fun listening experience. Use the provided script template to help guide you in crafting your report.

Finally, spread the joy! Once you've put together your happy news, share it with your family and friends. Doesn't it feel good to switch focus this way, and be a source of inspiration and hope rather than pessimism? This activity not only helps brighten your day, but also encourages those around you to focus on the good in the world, proving that sometimes, happiness is just a story away! This exercise is most powerful when tackled on those days you're feeling especially down or negative. Can you challenge yourself to find something worth celebrating instead?

Setting Radical Acceptance Goals

In today's productivity-obsessed world, it's easy to imagine that the only path towards happiness is to continually do more, be more, know more. But this can be an incredibly stressful state of mind to be in, creating a horizon that can never be reached. **What about fostering true contentment with *what is*, and acknowledging your life just as it is right now?**

Acceptance is often seen as a passive state, but in reality, it's a powerful tool for emotional resilience. Setting radical acceptance goals encourages you to embrace life as it is, without judgment or resistance. This practice helps you navigate challenges with greater ease, allowing you to focus on what you can control instead of getting caught up in frustration over what you can't.

To develop this skill, start by identifying goals for things you'd like to practice accepting. Not improving, developing, or cultivating, but simply accepting and embracing, just exactly as they are. Think about the small, medium, and big aspects of your life where acceptance can bring you some much-needed peace.

Let's begin with three small things you can radically accept. These might be everyday annoyances that tend to get under your skin. For instance, someone cutting in front of you in line for the bus can be annoying, but it's a small bump in the road. What are a few little irritations you can let go of?

Next, consider three medium things you can accept. Perhaps it's something like burning the food you were cooking. It's frustrating, but it happens to all of us. Reflect on moments that have caused you mild frustration and jot those down.

Finally, think about three big things—more significant, stressful situations that really test your ability to accept. Not getting the job you applied for can sting, but accepting it can also open up new opportunities. What are some larger challenges you can list?

If you wish to take this exercise even further, start to consider some general facts about life or your present circumstances that you cannot change, for example your body, your relationships, your limitations, or any other concrete realities in your life. Is there something you have been endlessly pushing against? Today's the day to experiment with simply accepting it for what it is.

By setting these radical acceptance goals, you can embrace the ride and find your balance amid the chaos. An enormous amount of stress disappears when we stop trying to resist reality!

Set Daily Intentions

A day without intention is like sailing a ship without a compass—you drift aimlessly, missing opportunities for growth and fulfillment. Even worse, you may find yourself caught up in someone or something else's intentions, and before you know it, your energy and attention have been hijacked. If you've ever watched a day become derailed by distractions, disruptions, or pointless digressions, then you'll know exactly how insidious a problem this can be.

Setting intentions can be incredibly beneficial, helping you cultivate a positive and proactive mindset that guides your daily actions and decisions. Intentions keep you sharp and alert. This practice encourages mindfulness and focus on the present moment, ultimately leading to improved mental health and a stronger sense of purpose. If you can pay attention only to what's important, then you are not bothered or stressed by everything else that is *not* important. Your anxiety levels go down.

So, how do you set intentions and goals effectively? Start by reflecting on what truly matters to you. For intentions, think about the kind of person you want to be and the values you want to embody. Practices like meditation or journaling can help keep these intentions at the forefront of your mind.

When it comes to goals, consider the specific achievements or milestones you wish to reach. Write them down in clear, positive language, and create a step-by-step plan with actionable steps to get there. For example, "I am a good father and husband. I value family and service, and want to dedicate myself to modelling a healthy life for my children. Specifically, this means maintaining good discipline at home, but also, I want to get that promotion to teach my kids about the power of hard work. Today, that means getting up when the alarm goes off and starting with my most difficult tasks first, when my mind is freshest. Today, my intention is to be disciplined and do what I say I will."

Ask yourself:

What do I value?

Who am I and who do I want to be?

What are my long-, medium- and short-term goals?

Given my values and goals, what is my intention for today?

How do I want to be today?

What do I want to do today?

It's important to regularly review and adjust both your intentions and goals to ensure they stay aligned with your evolving aspirations and life circumstances. This ongoing reflection can enhance your motivation and overall well-being.. At the end of the week, take some time to reflect on what happened, assess your progress, and adjust your intentions as needed.

Inspirational Quote Cryptogram

Sometimes, finding inspiration can be tough, but you can uncover it by decoding it! The inspiring quotes cryptogram is a unique mental health activity designed for seeking both fun and motivation. This engaging exercise challenges you to decode encrypted messages containing uplifting quotes from renowned thinkers, blending entertainment with wisdom.

Start by visiting the Puzzle Maker website (https://puzzlemaker.discoveryeducation.com/cryptogram) or similar to help you create a fun cryptogram. Enter your favorite anxiety-busting quote, for example the one from Dan Millman:

"You don't have to control your thoughts. You just have to stop letting them control you." Create your puzzle and, if you can, print out the result. Then, solve the puzzle! Each letter in the phrase is replaced with a random letter or number, and your task is to decode the message.

As you work through the codes, you'll not only stimulate your critical thinking and problem-solving skills, you'll also connect with powerful, encouraging messages that can enhance your mood and perspective. You deliberately slow down and give yourself time to properly meditate on the messages in the quote–while having some fun, too.

Puzzles like this can also serve as a calming practice, providing a mental break that allows you to focus your thoughts and reduce anxiety. The act of decoding engages your mind, helping to shift your focus away from stressors and toward a productive, creative task.

Each quote offers an opportunity for reflection, allowing you to internalize the wisdom behind the words as you crack the code. This activity transforms the process of decoding into a mental health exercise, reminding you that inspiration can often be found in unexpected places. When you're done, you may even have a piece of artwork that you can incorporate into another exercise or paste into your journal or diary.

Engaging with this puzzle not only boosts your mood, but also provides a moment of tranquility, proving that a little decoding can spark your inspiration while soothing your mind! Plus, as you share your favorite quotes with friends or family, you create connections and inspire others, spreading positivity further and amplifying the benefits of this enriching experience.

Exploring My Values

When we don't know our values, we can feel a bit lost, wandering through life without a clear sense of direction. We might set goals and work hard, but what's the *point* of all that hard work? What is it all in service of? Without knowing what we truly stand for, we may understandably feel a little aimless in life. This may manifest as disinterest, procrastination, lack of motivation, or anxiety.

One effective way to uncover what truly matters to you is by looking back at the values held by those around you—family, friends, and society. Take a moment to reflect on the values that have been passed down to you and consider how they align with your own beliefs and aspirations. It's about *actively and deliberately* considering your position, rather than just going along with momentum.

Start by examining your parents' values.

- *What principles did they instill in you?*

- *What principles didn't they instill?*
- *In what ways are your values different from theirs?*

Next, think about someone you respect or admire.

- *What values do they embody?*
- *What exactly is it about them that you most like?*

You may also consider someone you actively dislike, disrespect, or even fear.

- *What values does this person embody?*
- *What values do they clearly NOT have?*
- *What does your dislike of them tell you about what you value as a person?*

Finally, think about society and your cultural world as a whole.

- *What values are held highest in your world?*
- *In what ways do you agree with these values?*
- *In what ways do you disagree?*

This exercise encourages you to explore society's norms and expectations, helping you discern what resonates with you personally. Too often we either absorb everything our society imbues in us, or we reject it entirely. Realistically, however, a little discernment may be necessary to uncover the shades of gray and nuances.

Reflecting on these influences not only provides insight into your own values, but also inspires and affirms your sense of self. Recognizing what you truly value can empower you to make choices that align with your beliefs, fostering a greater sense of fulfillment. **By identifying the values you wish to live by, you can set intentions for how you want to navigate your life moving forward.** Try to clearly separate your needs and goals from those of people around you.

Ultimately, this process of exploration encourages a deeper understanding of yourself, promoting self-acceptance and resilience as you align your actions with your values. As you fill out the worksheet, you'll find clarity and motivation to pursue a life that reflects who you are at your core.

Personal Mantra

We've reiterated this basic truth in many different ways: **what you say to yourself matters.** That's why it's worth being intentional and deliberate about self-talk, and the kinds of words and sentiments you expose yourself to.

A mantra can be a powerful tool for shaping your mindset and fostering personal growth. Think of it as your own personal rallying cry, a way to remind yourself of your goals and aspirations. Not only do you continually pull your attention to an object of your own choosing, but you repeatedly reinforce a particular emotion and state of mind by doing so.

In this activity, you'll create a simple personal mantra that reflects your unique desires and aspirations. This practice is rooted in the belief that we are the architects of our own lives, capable of manifesting change through our thoughts and intentions. **It starts with words– and the power behind those words.**

Repeating your mantra regularly can help reinforce positive beliefs and propel you toward your highest self. Your mantra should resonate deeply with *you*, which means it doesn't have to make sense to anyone else. For instance, you might choose something like, "I will create positive change," or "I'm choosing happiness." The key is to ensure your mantra is authentic and meaningful to you, your goals, and your values. What you *don't* want to do is merely repeat the words without tapping into the meaning behind them.

To get started, spend 10-15 minutes distraction-free with your journal. Plan this time in the morning when your mind is fresh. Free-write about what you desire now, allowing your thoughts to flow without judgment. Afterward, review your journaling and identify what resonates most with you; it may be helpful to circle or highlight the words or phrases that stand out.

Once you've done this, decide which idea, goal, concept, or emotion you want to focus on first. Turn it into a declarative statement. For example, if you want financial security, write, "I have everything I need to live abundantly." It's a good idea to phrase your mantras in the positive, present tense, for example, "I am calm and content" rather than "I will be calm and content" or "I will not be stressed and anxious."

To incorporate your mantra into your daily routine, build 5-10 minutes into your schedule for quiet time to focus and repeat your mantra to yourself. This can be during moments of stillness, whether you're sitting, walking, or commuting. Again, write your mantra down. That way, you can repeat it to yourself every time it catches your eye.

DIY Daily Quote Calendar

Our negative, anxious thoughts are embedded into our cognitive habits like ruts worked into the ground. To overcome them, we need to consistently create healthier, happier alternatives, and repeat them over and over until they become more automatic, replacing the old habits. In other words, **when it comes to cultivating a healthy, anxiety-free mindset, repetition is important.**

There are days when people feel uninspired or drained, making a little motivation essential. For many, a great quote can flip a lackluster day into something uplifting and energizing.

That's where the DIY quote calendar comes in—a creative way to curate daily inspiration. This enjoyable project allows you to craft a personalized collection of quotes that resonate with them. Every moment spent in this frame of mind gently reshapes your mental habits bringing you closer to the person you want to be.

To start, gather a few supplies: scissors or a paper cutter, colorful cardstock or construction paper, and your favorite markers. Begin by cutting out 365 squares, each representing a day of the year. Choose colors that you love, which will make the project visually appealing.

Next, label each square with the corresponding date, using a calendar to ensure everything is accurate. After the dates are sorted, think about the special occasions and holidays you want to remember, jotting those down as well.

Now for the exciting part: it's time to fill each square with inspiring quotes! Select quotes that motivate or uplift you, whether they're from famous figures or personal mantras. Include mottos and mantras from other exercises in this book, compliments you've received, or even single word phrases that remind you of your values and intentions. Include phrases and terms that you'd like to gradually incorporate into your own positive self-talk, such as "You can do it!" or "One day at a time." You could even include relevant images and symbols, if you're feeling creative.

Once you've written down your quotes, arrange the squares in chronological order, placing January 1 at the top and December 31 at the bottom. Now you're all set to use your creation! Each day, pull out a square to read the quote and let it inspire you. This DIY project not only adds a burst of positivity to your workspace, but also makes for thoughtful gifts for friends and loved ones.

With a touch of creativity, you'll have a year's worth of motivation right at your fingertips! Why not try this activity at the close of December, so you have something fun to look forward to for the year ahead?

Developing Patience

Have you ever considered the relationship between anxiety and patience?

Patience is a handy tool for combating stress, but let's face it: some people just aren't wired to be patient. In a fast-paced world where immediate gratification is the norm, it's easy to feel overwhelmed. We may simply get into the habit of continually dialing up the pace without ever pausing to consider, "What's the rush?"

Developing patience can significantly enhance your well-being and help you manage stress more effectively. It begins with identifying situations that trigger impatience. Start by writing down specific scenarios that make you feel rushed or frustrated, allowing you to pinpoint moments where patience tends to wane. For each situation, note in your journal the thoughts associated with those feelings. Ask yourself:

When last did I feel impatient, rushed, or overwhelmed?

What exactly caused me to feel this way?

What thoughts, beliefs, and assumptions accompanied this impatient feeling?

Are there other times in life where I have felt that way?

Next, challenge those thoughts by considering a different perspective. Ask yourself: Is there a more constructive way to view this situation? This shift in perspective can help mitigate impatience. Then, list mindfulness techniques you can use for each scenario. Mindfulness practices, like deep breathing or simply pausing to observe your surroundings, can cultivate a greater sense of calm.

Finally, reflect on your tendency to seek immediate gratification. Start practicing delaying gratification in small ways, like waiting a few extra minutes before checking your phone or enjoying a treat. Set specific goals for practicing patience, such as focusing on your breath during stressful moments or choosing to wait before reacting in situations that provoke impatience.

Sometimes, we can get caught up in beliefs, expectations and assumptions that then lead us to anxious feelings. For example, we may tell ourselves "I have to get this done right now!" but on closer inspection, is that really true? Instead of getting upset, it may be an opportunity to practice patience and acceptance: "I'd like this to get done now, but it's not the end of the world if it doesn't."

Having patience as a skill enriches personal experiences, enhances relationships, and affirms your overall resilience and commitment to self-improvement.

When Was I (Not) Resilient?

Resilience is the ability to bounce back from challenges and setbacks, and it's an essential skill that helps us navigate life's ups and downs. It is equally important to recognize moments when you've displayed resilience and moments where you didn't. Answering the questions "When was I resilient? When was I not?" is the goal of this exercise. It will help you to reflect on moments when you coped well, as well as moments when you struggled.

Sometimes, we have far more resilience than we think. Other times, we can offer ourselves more support and help if only we have a little more awareness about where we have actually struggled. It comes down to honestly and compassionately appraising both our strengths and weaknesses.

In your journal, start by thinking about a situation where you demonstrated resilience. What was going on at that time? Take a moment to jot down the context and the resilience qualities you could tap into, like perseverance or self-confidence. What helped you access those strengths? What skills, perspectives, or approaches helped you overcome the challenge? Recognizing how these qualities contributed to your success can highlight the power of resilience in your life. **Remind yourself that you can be strong!**

Now, let's shift gears and consider a time when you didn't feel so resilient. What was the situation? What qualities of resilience were you unable to access? **With kindness and understanding, try to figure out exactly where you fell short, and why.** It's important to reflect on what prevented you from drawing on those strengths, and to think about the consequences of that moment. Understanding these experiences can provide valuable insights for your potential response during tough times in the future.

Finally, take a moment to reflect on both scenarios. Picture yourself in the first situation—what words would you use to describe how you felt? What identity were you carrying with you? Then, do the same for the second scenario. How can you transfer a little of the resilience you have into those areas that still need some work? This reflection can shed light on your resilience, showing you areas where you've grown and aspects you might want to work on. No matter what that looks like for you, try to accept and embrace yourself, just as you are.

Doing this exercise affirms your ability to learn and grow from every experience, while acknowledging that improvement is always possible. Recognizing your strengths alongside your challenges reinforces the understanding that **resilience is not just about toughing it out but about embracing your journey, flaws, and all.**

Cultivating Realistic Optimism

When we suffer from anxiety, it can sometimes feel like we are not pessimists, but "realists." From our perspective, looking on the bright side can seem hopelessly naïve. But is that really a fair appraisal?

Realistic optimism **is the belief that success is within reach through hard work and thoughtful planning, all while keeping a positive outlook on life's challenges.** It's a balanced, healthy perspective on life that's all about expecting good things to happenwhile also being prepared for whatever hurdles may come your way. Think of it as a "best of both worlds" mental strategy.

The realistic optimism activity invites you to dive deeper into this concept by reflecting on meaningful stories that showcase realistic optimism. Whether it's a personal experience or a tale shared by someone else, think about how maintaining a positive perspective can actually help you—or others—overcome life's obstacles. As you jot down these narratives, consider how they embody the essence of positive thinking, preparing for challenges, and the magic of reframing difficulties into learning experiences. What you're doing, essentially, is deliberately looking for counterevidence that pessimism and anxiety is always the most intelligent or rational approach. To get you started, Think about a particular pessimistic belief you may have, such as "nice guys always finish last." See if you can deliberately turn this on its head, for example, "nice guys often come out on top." Next, deliberately seek out stories or anecdotes that prove this new sentiment to be true.

If it helps, imagine you are literally arguing against your pessimistic self. Is there a story out there where the positive expectations turned out to be the most correct and logical one? **How does it feel to focus on this story, rather than the pessimistic one?**

This exercise is an opportunity for you to recognize and articulate moments when you or those around you demonstrated realistic optimism. Reflect on how these stories can remind you of your own resilience and strength. Life will always throw challenges your way, but a positive mindset and a proactive approach can turn those challenges into stepping stones for growth and success.

Engaging in this activity affirms your capacity to navigate tough times with grace. It's a reminder that setbacks are just part of your journey, and with the right mindset, you can transform obstacles into opportunities. By reflecting on these stories you not only enhance your understanding of realistic optimism, you also inspire yourself to embrace it in your own life, empowering you to face whatever comes next with renewed confidence and hope.

Protective Factors

Protective factors are the elements in our lives that help bolster mental health and build resilience, enabling us to navigate challenges more effectively. When you have a strong set of protective factors—such as nurturing relationships and effective coping skills—you're typically better equipped to handle whatever life throws your way.

When we struggle with anxiety, we can forget that, although life has its challenges, we are in possession of tools and techniques to help us navigate these challenges. **Life is full of problems, but it's also full of solutions.**

The protective factors exercise is designed to help you identify and enhance these essential elements, and start to remind yourself of all the useful tools and strategies you have at your disposal.

Take a moment to reflect in your journal on the supportive relationships you have, the coping strategies that work for you, and the personal skills that empower you. Then, you can use your answers to think about how you want to improve these factors moving forward.

Think about each of the following areas and rate them on a scale of 1 – 10:

- Social support
- Coping skills
- Sense of purpose and direction
- Physical health
- Mental and cognitive health
- Self-esteem

Next, ask yourself:

- Which area needs most work right now?
- Which area has been most beneficial?
- What protective factors would you like to develop further?
- What protective factors may you be under-using currently?
- What can you do today to more effectively draw on protective factors you already possess?

This activity is not just about self-reflection; it's also a fantastic opportunity to set specific goals that can inform your personal growth and treatment plans. By engaging with this worksheet, you affirm your capacity for change and resilience. Recognizing and nurturing your protective factors not only strengthens your ability to cope with difficulties, but also enhances your sense of self-worth and confidence. As you identify the resources you have at your disposal, you're reminded of your inner strength and your ability to thrive, reinforcing the belief that you *can* overcome challenges and lead a fulfilling life. In fact, you've probably already done so many times in the past!

IMPROVE the moment

When we're stuck in an anxiety spiral, sometimes there's nothing we can do but ride out those feelings and wait for calm to return. That's where the IMPROVE the moment exercise comes into play. This tool introduces a range of Dialectical Behavior Therapy (DBT) skills designed to promote emotion regulation and coping during tough times. **The acronym IMPROVE stands for Imagery, Meaning, Prayer, One thing in the moment, Vacation, and Encouragement,** making it easy to recall these skills when they are needed most.

IMPROVE the Moment
distress tolerance skills

Distressing situations do not always have quick solutions. When this is the case, there might be no choice but to sit with uncomfortable emotions and wait for them to pass. The **IMPROVE** acronym outlines skills for *improving the moment*, making it easier to tolerate these situations.

I — Imagery
Imagine a peaceful place far from your worries. What are the sights, sounds, and smells you notice? Alternately, vividly envision the best possible resolution of your current challenge.
Use each sense to imagine relaxing on a beach.   Visualize a stressful conversation going well.

M — Meaning
Is there any meaning you can find or create from your situation? Reflect on ways you can use your current experience to gain insight or help others.
Name any positive aspects of your struggle.   List the ways you can grow from this experience.

P — Prayer
Use prayer to accept what you cannot control or seek guidance on navigating a difficult situation. Connect with a higher power or your own wise mind.
Say a prayer.   Repeat a mantra.   List five things you're grateful for.   Meditate.

R — Relaxation
Find a quiet place where you can practice a relaxation technique of your choice. If you notice your attention wandering back to your worries, gently bring it back to your practice.
Practice deep breathing.   Use progressive muscle relaxation.   Stretch.   Practice yoga.

O — One thing in the moment
Immerse yourself in a simple or repetitive activity that requires your full engagement. This could be a household chore or a mental task like counting or memorizing.
Pull weeds.   Organize your clothes.   Memorize a poem.   Count backward from 100.

V — Vacation
Take a short break from your worries and do something fun or nourishing. This can refresh you and lead to a fresh perspective when you resume your day.
Call a good friend.   Go on hike.   Read something that interests you.   Watch a favorite movie.

E — Encouragement
Practice being your own best advocate by repeating words of support to yourself. Be sure to select a phrase that feels authentic and motivates you to keep going.
"I got this!"   "This too shall pass."   "I survived before, and I'll survive again."   "I'll be OK."

Provided by TherapistAid.com © 2022 Therapist Aid LLC

Using the guide above (courtesy of Therapist Aid, 2022), move through each letter of the acronym the next time you're feeling overwhelmed with anxiety. You may find that, depending on how you feel, certain letters/activities are more helpful than others, and that's OK. One option is to print this sheet out and keep it at hand–there's bound to be at least one prompt that can act as a life raft in a difficult situation.

Working with this acronym not only affirms your capacity to handle challenges, but also encourages you to cultivate healthier emotional responses. It fosters a sense of resilience and self-compassion, empowering you to navigate those uncomfortable moments with greater ease. By applying these strategies, you'll find yourself better equipped to face difficulties and emerge even stronger, transforming obstacles into opportunities for personal growth and deeper self-awareness. Each time you engage with these skills, you're building a toolkit that can support you throughout life's ups and downs, ultimately leading to a more balanced and fulfilling life

Positive Journaling

Positive journaling is different from gratitude journaling; it's about actively seeking out the positive moments in your day. Think of it as a little like "reverse complaining," or deliberately flexing your optimism muscle. Research shows that frequent journaling can significantly uplift your mood, making it a valuable practice for enhancing your overall well-being. **In time, the positive mindset reflected in those pages becomes more naturally internalized as your own.**

With a positive journal , you have the chance to reflect on your day and capture what truly made you happy. Each day, simply take a moment to write down three brief entries—just one sentence each—describing something positive that happened. It could be anything, as long as it made you feel good in some way. Remember, these entries don't need to be monumental; they can be as simple as enjoying a delicious meal or taking a calming walk.

This exercise is especially beneficial if you sometimes struggle to see the silver linings in your life. It serves as a gentle reminder to recognize and celebrate the good around you, which gently reorients your perspective to something healthier and more positive. Engaging in positive journaling helps affirm your ability to notice and appreciate the small joys, reinforcing the idea that even ordinary moments can bring happiness.

You can include small, positive journal entries simply by writing the date/day name at the top of the page, and listing out three things that were positive that day. Interestingly, you may find yourself listing things that are neutral–however, your attitude and perspective made them seem positive. For example:

1. You had your favorite cereal for breakfast
2. You had a really funny text exchange with an old friend you'd lost touch with
3. Your boss seemed genuinely impressed with an idea you shared

If you enjoy the writing process, feel free to expand on your entries. You can combine this style of journaling with many other expressive or exploratory journaling practices, too. For example, why not imagine the positive, grateful version of yourself writing a letter to the sometimes grumpy, pessimistic version of yourself? What would you say?

As you take the time to reflect on positive experiences, you'll cultivate a more optimistic mindset that can enhance your overall well-being. **You may find that your attitude changes somewhat, and that you go about your days actively *looking* for things to be happy and grateful about**–what a powerful antidote to anxiety and worry! This practice empowers you to shift your focus away from negativity and self-doubt, allowing you to appreciate the present and acknowledge your capacity for joy.

Remember: what you focus on expands in your awareness. As you fill your journal with these moments, you'll not only reinforce your resilience, but also create a personal narrative that highlights your strengths and the goodness in your life. Ultimately, this nurtures a deeper sense of self-worth and contentment within you.

Conclusion

Nobody would argue that life can be stressful at times. Overthinking and worry can get the better of us, and it's not uncommon to sometimes feel like we're struggling to reign in negativity, fearfulness, or worried thoughts. That said, there are countless simple, effective strategies out there for gaining greater self-awareness, calm, and confidence as you navigate life's inevitable challenges. No matter how you feel right now, these tools are always accessible to you, even if we only have ten minutes to spare.

One final exercise you can consider is this: Of all the activities presented here, which was your favorite, and why? If you had to add something, what would it be? The truth is, we are all blessed with the capacity to cope, to be resilient, and to make meaning of our experiences–you included! To finish our book, here is an invitation turn your focus inward and check in with your own wisdom. What do you know about anxiety, and how to overcome it? What valuable lessons have you learned on your journey? What advice are you best equipped to give to yourself?

The next time you're feeling overwhelmed by stress and worry, remind yourself of all this. In the words of Robert Trew, **"Trust yourself. You've survived a lot, and you'll survive whatever is coming."**

www.ingramcontent.com/pod-product-compliance
Lightning Source LLC
Chambersburg PA
CBHW060607080526
44585CB00013B/715